Anonymous

Glimpses of the Monastery: A Brief Sketch of the History of the Ursulines of Quebec. From 1739 to 1839

Part. 3

Anatiposi

Anonymous

Glimpses of the Monastery: A Brief Sketch of the History of the Ursulines of Quebec. From 1739 to 1839

Part. 3

Reprint of the original, first published in 1875.

1st Edition 2024 | ISBN: 978-3-38283-122-6

Anatiposi Verlag is an imprint of Outlook Verlagsgesellschaft mbH.

Verlag (Publisher): Outlook Verlag GmbH, Zeilweg 44, 60439 Frankfurt, Deutschland
Vertretungsberechtigt (Authorized to represent): E. Roepke, Zeilweg 44, 60439 Frankfurt, Deutschland
Druck (Print): Books on Demand GmbH, In de Tarpen 42, 22848 Norderstedt, Deutschland

GLIMPSES OF THE MONASTERY:

A

BRIEF SKETCH

OF THE

HISTORY OF THE URSULINES

OF

QUEBEC.

FROM 1739 TO 1839:

PART III.

𝔄. 𝔐. 𝔇. 𝔊.

QUEBEC:

PRINTED BY C. DARVEAU.

1875.

mutual delight. The Ursulines of Quebec shared the public rejoicings in no common degree. To their just appreciation of their pastor's merits on this first interview, they soon had occasion to add their gratitude for the many instances of his paternal interest in their welfare.

The Marquis de Beauharnais had governed the colony for the last fifteen years, and might well rejoice in the progress that had been made during his administration. All along the banks of the St. Lawrence, through more than a hundred parishes, he could point to thriving farms stocked with cattle, set with fruit-trees, and yielding fine harvests of grain, vegetables, and all the productions required for living comfortably. Within the snug cottage, the pleasant farm-house, and the Seigniorial manor, the busy wheel and industrious loom gave employment to female hands, supplying the household with clothing according to the season. Mines of copper and lead had been discovered along the lakes; the Iron Foundry of St. Maurice [1] had called the hidden metal from its ore, and now furnished implements of husbandry and cutlery for which the people had hitherto been dependent on France. The exports of Canada were no longer confined to peltry, but included the surplus products of the country, to which might be added the important resource of ship-building.

The good Bishop had reason to be equally satisfied with the religious aspect of his diocese, as far as Canada was concerned. Thirteen establishments of education, or of charity, published the zeal of his predecessors, and gave evidence of the spirit in which the Colony had been founded. In Quebec, science and letters had long been cultivated at the college of the Jesuits and at the Seminary of Bishop Laval. Montreal had the fine Seminary of the Sulpicians, to diffuse the blessings of learning and piety among its 3000 inhabitants.

As to the extent of the diocese and the

---

[1] Near Three-Rivers.

over these the pastoral solicitude of the Bishop would be exerted. The indefatigable missionaries continued their arduous labors, amid the innumerable obstacles presented by the roving life of our American aborigines. Sad to say, new obstacles had been put to their conversion : new vices had been awakened in these poor children of the forests, by the conduct of those vagrant hunters, *les coureurs de bois*,[1] who, trafficking in fur and ardent spirits, might well be called the missionaries of evil. Their lives and practices fully exemplified a saying of our venerable Mother Mary of the Incarnation, that "without the restraints of religion, a Frenchman would soon lay aside those of civilization and become worse than a savage."

Such then—in a few words—was the

---

[1] This roving life had such attractions that laws had to be made to prevent the absence of so many young Frenchmen from the Colony. No fewer than 800, were, at one time, thus absent without leave.— *Hist. of Can.*

aspect of this vast country, confided for
its spiritual wants to the care of Bishop
de Pontbriand, in 1741; such had it become in the space of a century, counting
from that feeble commencement, that
weak infancy in which it appeared when
our Venerable Mother, with her heroic
companions, first set foot upon its soil.

The expiration of another century
[1839] will present a still greater contrast;
yet we shall see that through all its vicissitudes and through all its trials, from within or from without, Canada has, thus far,
been " a country especially guarded by
Divine Providence. [1] "

[1] Words of Ven. Mère Marie de l'Incarnation.

CHAPTER II.

THE URSULINES IN 1739.

.

Revisiting the cloister, where, in 1739, Rev. Mother Migeon of the Nativity occupies the first place, in a Community of fifty one [1] nuns, we naturally enquire who are the " ancients ; " for to them, as to the " Elders of the people," we look for the preservation of the chain of tradition. To them it belongs to keep alive the primitive spirit of the foundresses, and to transmit the same, unchanged, to succeeding generations.

Five worthy Mothers whose ages range from sixty-six to seventy-seven — all of whom have made the Monastery their

---

[1] 37 choir nuns and 14 lay-sisters. See Glimpses, Part II, p. 243, &c.

home for the last half century—are introduced to us in answer to our demand, as follows :—

Mother Madeleine Amiot of the Conception.

Mother Louise-Rose de Lanaudière of St. Catherine.

Mother Marie-Anne · Robineau of the Holy Trinity.

Mother Marie Madeleine Drouard of St. Michel, Assistant.

Mother Marie-Jeanne Chorel of St. Ursula.

The name of Mother Amiot of the Conception carries us far back into the preceding century.—She entered the Convent (1677) only five years after the decease of our Ven. Mother Mary of the Incarnation ; and when her own death occurred in 1747, she had seen seventy summers within the cloister. She had lived twenty-four years with Mother St. Ignatius, (Miss Charlotte Barré,) eighteen with that first Parisian Superior, Mother

St. Athanasius; and forty with Rev. Mother Le Maire des Anges.

She is named among the foundresses of the Ursulines of Three Rivers; and during her long career of usefulness here in Quebec, she was called, at various times, to fill the most laborious as well as the highest offices.

Let us, dear reader, rest a few moments in the company of this venerated Mother Amiot of the Conception, who has spent the greater part of her days in the shadow of the sanctuary, and see what her example will teach us.

Our Annals picture her in the freshness of "sweet thirteen," an only child, led by her fond mother into the midst of those brilliant circles of pleasure which constituted the fashionable world of Quebec at that time; yet despising the vain show and rejecting the allurements of society as an unworthy slavery, while as yet her inexperience could not have fathomed the void, nor suspected the dangers of the cup that was presented her.

Permitted, at her earnest request, to re-
enter the Convent as boarder, her in-
stinctive disgust for the world serves as
a preparation for the grace of a special
attraction for the things of God ; and before the completion of her fifteenth year,
she has obtained for her portion the liberty of the servants of Jesus-Christ, the
privilege to adopt his Cross as her only
inheritance.

From the day she is clothed with the
livery of the Spouse of Christ to that later
period when she wears lightly the burthen
of her fourscore years, she sheds around
her the sweet odor of edification, the bright
and shining example of every virtue.

Need we follow her from year to year
through the various labors assigned her
in the house of God ? Here all offices
are of the same value when their duties
are fulfilled with equal perfection : her
talents fitted her for all, and her piety
rendered all sweet and profitable to herself and to the Community.

Now we behold her as the special advocate of the devotion to the Sacred Heart

of Jesus, winning souls to love Him by
words of burning zeal, while she writes
out the billets of the Association and ins-
cribes the long Register of names from
the time it is opened [1700] to her dying
day; now, with what alacrity she occupies
herself in adorning the Altar dedicated to
that sweet mystery! or, passing to the
Chapel of Saints, even in the severest of
the wintry season, she decorates, with
filial care, the shrine of Our Lady of Great
Power.

Now, become the most aged in the
community, we find her working with
her needle as deftly as at the age
of fifteen, fitting in the shades of silk,
as if with colors from the nicest painter's palette ; or wreathing, for some
country church, leaves and flowers into
such tasteful sprays as could be surpassed only by nature herself. Then,
the younger nuns press around her, won
as much by her grace and affability, as
by her exquisite skill. How often, while
guiding their willing fingers to round the
opening moss-rose, or spread the dazzling

petals of the lily, would the good Mother describe the Church of Madame de la Peltrie, and the altars once decorated by Mother Mary of the Incarnation, relating many an unwritten trait of those "good old times." How often would she express her deep conviction of the heroic sanctity of the venerable Mother, adding an ardent wish to see her name on the list of canonized Saints. That was, indeed, the frequent subject of her conversations with her Sisters, and the unvarying object of her prayers. "The zeal and the talents of Mother Amiot of the Conception, would have rendered her a fit instrument in promoting the cause of the canonization, had the times been more propitious for such an undertaking."[1]

In concluding her Obituary, the Annalist remarks : "Although our dear Mother Mary of the Conception was eighty-five years old, she had none of the usual infirmities of that advanced age. We had hoped to preserve her among us a few

[1] Letter of Mother St. Helen.

years longer, but she was ripe for heaven. Our Blessed Lord, whom she had so often crowned with flowers in the Sacrament of his love, wished to crown her with glory in his kingdom."

Have our readers recognized in Mother de Lanaudiere of St. Catherine, one of the two novices who commenced their career after the second restoration of the Monastery, by taking the veil in that temporary chapel beneath the community-Hall in 1688 ? [1] Mother St. Catherine, and Mother Robineau of the Trinity have yet to celebrate their Golden Jubilee, and to live to see the 76th year of their age, bearing cheerfully their share of the yoke of the Lord during the whole course of their long pilgrimage.

Mother Drouard of St. Michel prolongs her vigorous existence to the age of eighty-two, completing her 67th year in religion. Having obeyed the call of Heaven at the age of fourteen, she corresponded to this first grace, and after living the life of a

[1] See Glimpses, Part II, p. 46.

good and holy religious she dies with all the marks of predestination, in 1756.

Mother Chorel of St. Ursula [1674–1745] meets us as one who walks constantly in the presence of God, her happy memory enriched with the maxims and the doings of the Saints : her tender piety is the solace of long years of suffering and infirmity.

. Historical records enable us here to foretell that among the remaining thirty-two choir nuns in this Community of 1739, there are fifteen who will celebrate their Golden Jubilee : of these, ten will see the 60th, and some the 70th anniversary of their religious profession. The three novices of the white veil, Sister Davanne of St. Louis de Gonzague, Sr. Richard of St. Augustin, and Sr. Lagère of St. Gabriel are also candidates for the same honors.

These festivals, dear reader, are, in the Monastery, the counterpart of the Golden Wedding in the world. They have not required the formalities of a special legislation. The heart alone has dictated the programme ; and the Golden Jubilee of a religious profession is wont to be celebrated in a very joyous manner.

The good nun who has to review the mercies, the blessings and graces of half a century, enters upon the exercises of a Retreat, eight days previous to the recurring anniversary. Measuring the much she has received with the little she has given, she will place herself at the foot of the Tabernacle, in a spirit of penitence and humility ;—yet, over every other sentiment will rise the burden of the Psalmist's song : " What shall I render to my God for all his gifts to me ? " *Quid retribuam !*

As to the part which all the other members of the Community take in these rejoicings, it is one of the most precious occasions for the manifestation of fraternal charity. All is spontaneous, all is cordiality, sincere and unaffected, the impersonation of those glowing words : " Behold how good and how pleasant it is to dwell together in unity ! "

CHAPTER III.

PRIMITIVE TIMES AND MANNERS :·

CANADIAN SEIGNIORS. MISS ROBINEAU DE
BECANCOUR; MISS DE BOUCHERVILLE.

Associated with the names of our ancient Mothers, there often rises a charming
picture of the life and manners of those
primitive times, of which the Canadian
people are so justly proud.

Thus in the group that has just engaged our attention, Mother Marie-Anne
Robineau of the Trinity recalls to mind
the stately manor and the wide domains
which constituted the Baronies of Becancour and Portneuf. The seigniorial
mansion and chapel of stone, bearing the
insignia of nobility, were surrounded by
all the buildings required for a large retinue of servants, horses, and equipages;
there were besides the spacious farm-yard,
the parks, and the never-failing grist-mill.
The worthy Baron enjoyed by royal pa-

tent, " the right of arms, heraldry honors, rank and precedence, like the other barons of the kingdom of France ; his vassals," &c., yet, with his high prerogatives, the aged Seignior led a life which the historian Charlevoix, when receiving hospitality at the manor, likened to that of "the ancient patriarchs, sharing the labors of agriculture with his vassals, and living as frugally as they."

Perhaps the absence of his daughter had diminished the gayety of the household, for according to our traditions, Mother Robineau of the Trinity, during the three years she had passed under the paternal roof, had been afforded an ample share of amusements, dress, dancing, and the usual round of fashionable pastimes. The souvenir of these gay soirées, which she used to call gay follies, was not of a nature to inspire her with regret ; she could only despise the tyranny of custom which could induce people to " pass the whole night in bowing and courtesying —as in the ancient minuet—in the midst of a brilliantly illuminated hall."

Her own memory has come down to us with far sweeter associations. Mother Anne of the Trinity, in the Monastery, was the personification of fervent piety. When we read that "during forty years she retained, at her own request, the office of ringing the bell to awaken the Community at four o'clock," we feel that we need not pursue her Notice further to know " what spirit she was of."

Let us bring before us next, another picture of the olden times, in the family of our ancient and venerated Mother Genevieve Boucher de Boucherville, in religion, Mother St. Pierre.

Here we find something more intimate to contemplate; it is the secret intentions, the very heart of the ancient Governor of Three Rivers, the Honorable Pierre Boucher, who seems to us one of the noblest types of the Christian gentleman. For his probity and disinterestedness, his valor and merit, he had been endowed by the French monarch with titles of nobility, and a grant of an important tract of land along the St. Lawrence. The question with this dignitary, who was the father of a large family, was whether to remain in Three Rivers or to go and settle on his lands.

The project has been meditated at leisure and the motives for adopting it are written down. The questions were not : "How many thousands of dollars will this speculation bring me ? Are the risks balanced by the probabilities of success ?" nor any of the usual calculations in similar circumstances. We read—and feel instructed as we read—as follows :—

" I have determined to settle my lands of Boucherville for the following reasons; and I write them in order never to forget the motives that have influenced my determination, and the engagements to which I pledge myself.

" I wish also my successors to know my intentions and fulfil them, unless indeed they can do more for the glory of God.

"1º It is in order that there may be a place where the inhabitants, living in peace and harmony, may serve God sincerely, without fear of being troubled or molested.

" 2ª That I may live more retired from the world and its vain amusements, which only make us forget God ; and thus more conveniently labor to assure my own salvation and that of my family.

" 3° That I may by the most lawful means, increase my riches, provide for my family, and procure for my children a good and virtuous education, befitting the state of life which they may embrace.

" 4° The land being mine, I think it my duty to go and settle it, as a means of being useful to society.

" 5° In order to have the means of doing more good to my neighbor, and aiding those who are in want than I am able to do in my present position [Gov. of T. R.], where my revenue is insufficient for the goods works I wish to perform.

" For the success of my undertaking, I place my trust in God, begging his faithful servant Rev. Father de Brebeuf[1] to protect me in my attempt, if it be for the glory of God and the salvation of my family ; if otherwise, I pray that I may not succeed, desiring nothing but to accomplish the will of Heaven."

With intentions so pure and elevated, the noble Christian resigned to another the post of Governor, and removed to his new domain. The ample benedictions of Heaven were poured down on the rising settlement, and on every member of the pious household. Of fifteen children who surrounded the table of the *Seigneur de Boucherville*, two sons embraced the ecclesiastical state, and served God in his sanctuary with zeal and fidelity : one daughter consecrated herself to God as an Ursuline ; it was Genevieve, the eleventh child,—the one who, according to the father's testimony "loved him the best ; " and who, in fact, seems to have resembled him most in character.

[1] This holy Jesuit missionary was put to death in the most cruel manner by the Iroquois, 1649.

While his eldest son continues the succession and title of de Boucherville, his daughters present us, by their matrimonial alliances, the honorable names of de Grandpré, de Grosbois, de Montbrun, de Laperière, de Niverville, de Varennes, de Muy, de Sabrevois, and Le Gardeur.

Another document, portraying the heart of the venerable progenitor of the de Bouchervilles, who died in 1717, at the age of ninety-five, in the odor of sanctity, has been preserved to posterity, and is known as the "Legacy of Grandfather Boucher."[1]

We shall cite a few lines only, for this spiritual Testament is long: each member of the noble patriarch's family is addressed in turn, while the wisest counsels mingle with the effusions of paternal affection. Like another Tobias giving his dying blessing, he concludes, saying to all :—

[1] Not many years ago, according to the testimony of the Hon. J. Viger, of Montreal, this document was read annually, on the anniversary of the old patriarch's death, in presence of the assembled family, all *kneeling*.

"Love each other sincerely for the love of God; remember that you will one day be called, like, me to appear before God to render an account of your actions; hence do nothing of which you will later have to repent............. ....

...I do not leave you great riches, but what I have, has been honestly acquired. I would willingly have left you more, but God is the master of all things.

" I leave you many friends, persons of rank, honor and probity; I have no enemy, to my knowledge.

"I have done what lay in my power to live without reproach : do the same. Seek to render service to every one : disoblige no one, if you can oblige him without offending God.

" My children, ever keep before your eyes the fear of God, and seek to love him with your whole heart."

As to his wife, whom he recommends to the tenderest affection of his children, "his conscience reproaches him with

nothing that regards her, unless it be that
he has loved her too much ; but if that
has been an excess, he does not think God
has been offended by it."

Finally, to his *dearest* daughter, our
Ursuline, he says :—

" Do not grieve when you hear of my
death ; but pray for me, and rejoice that
God in calling me to himself, has delivered
me from the miseries of the present life.
If you have loved me more than the rest,
I also have had great affection for you,
and I shall have throughout eternity."

Then, as a dying souvenir, he bequeaths
to her a silver reliquary which he wears
upon his bosom, in these words : " It is
all that remains to me to give : it is but
just that I bestow it upon one who has
shown me so much affection."

These last words may strike some as
remarkable : the old patriarch evidently
does not share the opinion of such persons as accuse a daughter who conse-
crates herself to God of being wanting
in filial piety.

A long life of ninety-four years, ac-
corded to our beloved Mother St. Pierre,
seventy-two of which she passed in the
cloister, would furnish many edifying details; but a few lines will suffice to cha-
racterize her as the worthy daughter of
the *Grand père Boucher de Boucherville.*

According to the Annals: " Her only
ambition was to render herself agreeable
to her Divine Spouse by a strict observance of the rule, and all the duties of the
religious state; her silence and recollection, her piety, obedience, humility, and
poverty, rendered her a model for her
Sisters. Having abandoned the wealth
and honors of her family to follow Jesus-
Christ, she attached herself inviolably to
Him, seeking his sacramental presence on
the Altar, and in holy Communion, as
her chief and only delight. She served
the Community with equal fervor, and to
the satisfaction of all, whether employed
in the highest or the lowest offices."

Should any one inquire here, what has
become of the ancient domain of Pierre

De Boucherville, we should direct him to an aristocratic little village on the south shore of the St. Lawrence, a short distance below Montreal. There, the honorable descendants of the Ex-Governor of Three-Rivers, the first Seignior of Boucherville, have clustered their comfortable residences ; still keeping up much of the urbanity, the courteous and lofty demeanor, of the feudal lords of the age of Louis XIV. From the irregularly built hamlet, with its Church, its presbytery, its Convent and Chapel, its school-house, &c., we behold in the distance, Mount Boucherville, from the foot of which well two small streams, that spread fertility along their path, pausing at one point, to turn the necessary but noisy grist-mill.

Throughout the whole length and breadth of the ancient Governor's patrimony—an area of twenty-four square miles—appear pleasant country-seats, surrounded with gardens and orchards ; white cottages, half buried in verdure ; bright fields of wheat, oats, and maize, alternating with patches of forest trees, meadows and pasture lands.

In front of the village flow the bright waters of the St. Lawrence, losing themselves along the shore among verdant islands, as beautiful to behold as they are convenient for arable and grazing purposes.

But why attempt to describe a spot which has many a rival along the pleasant banks of the St. Lawrence? —scenes that Fancy herself

" Would scarcely dream of : which one's eye must see,
To know how beautiful this world can be."

If we have dwelt with complacency, as it were, upon the souvenirs of the Seignior de Boucherville, it must be parloned us, when we explain, that besides his daughter Genevieve, three of his grand-daughters consecrated themselves to God in the Monastery of the Ursulines, during the life-time of their venerable ancestor. These were, Mother Margaret le Varennes of the Presentation, Mother Marie-Anne de Boucherville of St. Ignatius, and Mother Charlotte de Muy of St. Helen, each of whom endeared herself to her contemporaries, and edified them by the example of an humble, pious, and useful life. At a later period, our Register shows the names of four great-granddaughters of the patriarch of Boucherville, perpetuating in the Convent the amiable traditions of hereditary piety.

CHAPTER IV.

THE MUSES IN THE CLOISTER.

1752.

Curious old manuscripts, after escaping during a century or more the annual perils of the season of house-cleaning, the Vandalism of epochs of demolition and reparations,—sometimes suddenly come to light; and make us wish there had been some law to prevent the destruction of other similar documents, of little interest perhaps in themselves, yet precious as objects of curiosity, and useful in illustrating the past history of the Convent.

Before us is one of those ancient scrolls, which appears of some importance : it is dated August 23d, 1752, and introduces us to a little scene in the cloister, by which we may form some idea of what was expected of the pupils of the Ursulines in those days. We can only make a few extracts.

The occasion that brought the company together within the Convent-Halls is not specified; whatever it may have been, we find there present :—The Governor, the Marquis Duquesne de Menneville; the Bishop of Quebec, de Pontbriand ; the Intendant;—perhaps also the City Major, the Chevalier Lemoyne de Longueil, with Mademoiselle Charlotte de Grey, now Madame de Longueil, who was not accustomed to miss any opportunity of entering the Monastery.

The Superioress, whose duty it was to
receive these distinguished guests, was
Rev. Mother Genevieve Boucher of St.
Pierre, the venerable Mother being now
in her eightieth year. By her side, as
next in office, are Mother La Grange of
St. Louis, Mother Drouard of St. Michael;
Mother Migeon of the Nativity—the late
Superioress. Mother Wheelwright of the
Infant Jesus and Mother de Muy of St.
Helen were near; while with the pupils,
directing their movements, might be seen
some of the younger nuns;—Mother Mar-
chand of St. Etienne, Mother Davanne of
St. Louis de Gonzague, and her compan-
ion, Mother Richard of St.-Augustin.

If this was an Examination, the List of
Prizes is, unfortunately, missing. Another
list, however, enables us to repeople the
Hall with pupils.

Let us transcribe a few names, for we
are about to behold an Arcadian scene.
Here are the Misses Madeleine and Catherine de Brouague, daughters of the Intendant of the Labrador-coasts; the Misses

de Lery. de Boisclair, de Gannes, de Lu-
signan, des Meloises, La Force, Gabrielle
de la Jonquière, Ursule Baby, &c. Here
also are the grand-nieces of the venerable
Superioress, Miss Françoise de Boucherville and Miss Boucher de Grosbois; Miss
Louise de Muy and others:[1] but let these
suffice, for our personages await.

Behold them, as, in the light costume of
nymphs and shepherdesses, they issue
from a verdant and flowery grove at
the extremity of the Hall.

Advancing in front of the illustrious
guests, an ingenious prologue serves to
rivet the attention of the audience. But
listen to the youthful shepherdess, who

---

[1] Other pupils of that time : The Misses DuPlessis,
Le Duc, Couillard, Durocher, Rhodes, Berthelot, Le-
Mire, Girard, Baudoin, Le Vasseur (Louisbourg) the
Misses de Blainville, Varin, de Vincelot, de Chavigny,
du Four, Poulin, LeBlanc, Hertel de Rouville, St.Hu-
bert, Voyer, Aubert, Taschereau, Berment de la
Martinière, Bedard, Rabby, Roussel, De l'Isle, Phili-
bert, de Lantagnac, Channazard, St. Germain, de
Grey, Chauveau, the Misses Fleury d'Eschambault,
the Misses de Verchères, Nicolet, Douville, &c.

compliments the Governor in a graceful
Idyl, in which from time to time, join the
whole group;—a chorus fit to wake all
the echoes, from the City of Champlain
to the Laurentides.

Observe the opening :—

SOLO.—Strike now a livelier chord,
        Awake a loftier strain ;
        Behold ! 'tis a Duquesne :
        Welcome ! the noble Lord !
        If his brave sires of old
        To France preserved a throne,
        His sword—it is foretold—
        Shall here the same uphold ;—
        The glory all his own.

CHORUS.

            Let his great name,
            O'er hill and plain,
            Resound in song :
        Sweet pipe and tabor bring !
            Let the glad echoes ring,
        Pouring triumphal notes along.
            From o'er the main
            He comes—Duquesne—
            To guard the land ;
        First in true worth, first in command !

2d. Shepherdess.

'Our vows were not in vain,
A brighter day has come ;
Peace broods o'er every home,
And plenty decks the plain.
Our flocks secure may stray,
In pastures fresh and green :
Our foes, all in dismay,
Flee from the light of day,
When such a Chief is seen.

3d. Shepherdess.

Gay Shepherds, cease your song :
To Orpheus yield the lyre ;
He has celestial fire,
To him the notes belong.
Let him in strains sublime,
Exalt our Hero's fame,—
Spread it to every clime,
Enduring as Old Time,
And worthy of his name ! [1]

Evidently, mythological lore is in vogue in Quebec, in the 18th century. On this occasion the muse, it must be allowed, has not been sparing of incense. In addressing the Bishop, the tone is more filial;

---

[1] For a copy of the original see Note A at the end of the volume.

and while the admiration is not less, there is greater simplicity.

> With united heart and voice
> We sing our gratitude ;
> Our Pastor is of God's own choice,
> Beloved, as he is good !
> Unbounded is his sacred zeal,—
> His flock his only care ;
> No words his merit can reveal,
> Nor all our love declare.

Poems in honor of the worthy Bishop were recited on more than one occasion. During the course of that same year, the pious Prelate, "whose zeal for the good of souls left him no repose, was five months absent from Quebec, giving retreats at Montreal for the Religious Communities and for the public, as he had done here before his departure. He penetrated some forty or fifty leagues beyond Montreal, traversing pathless deserts, through marshes and ravines, borne over frightful rapids in a bark canoe ;—undergoing hardships that can scarcely be imagined. His return was celebrated by our poets

in many forms." The following version
shows a part of one of these Occasional
Odes :

1.

While peals of joy ring out to-day,
And happy crowds obstruct the way,
To bless our peaceful Convent-home,
Our worthy Prelate deigns to come.
My Lord, accept from children dear,
A tribute humbly yet sincere :
To sing of sacred zeal like thine,
The Muse herself should be divine.

2.

While thou wert absent all was dull,
Flora herself no flowers would cull :
The zephyrs fled our lonely bowers,
And slowly waned the weary hours.
One warbler sang ;—'twas Philomel,
Repeating what we know so well :—
To sing of sacred zeal like thine,
The Muse herself should be divine.

3.

Ah ! wonder not that all rejoice,
And greet thee with exulting voice,
Thrice honored Prelate, when 'tis known
What glorious works thy hand has done.

With admiration, all may see
The land, renewed in piety :—
O yes ! to sing of zeal like thine,
The Muse herself should be divine !

Our last specimen of the poetical effusions of the epoch, records also a historical
fact. It was in 1753. The Ursulines of
Three Rivers had seen their Convent destroyed by fire.[1] The worthy Prelate's
generous devotedness on that occasion,
was appreciated, not only by the imme-
diate objects of his benevolence, but also
by the Ursulines of Quebec.

We are careful to preserve the mythological allusions in our version. The
poem begins :—

Among the gods, if poets' lays are true,
A metamorphis was not rare to view ;
And all Olympus did the feat admire,
When bright Apollo cast aside his lyre,
Forbore to sing, and seized the heavy spade ;
Or with the mason's trowel, mortar laid.
Like him, my Lord, you put the apron on,
And soften hearts,—while you are laying stone.

[1] See Glimpses, Part II, p. 88.

More than Apollo's, we your labors prize,
While from their ruins sacred walls arise.
What charity is yours! what holy zeal!
How generous to promote the public weal!
God's glory is your aim ;—and here we find
A lesson, for ourselves to take to mind.
Our daily labors must, to Heaven, all tend :
God, and our neighbor's good, our only end.

Oh! Heaven has blest your mission, all of love.
And guards for you the brightest crown above!
Long may it be our happy lot to know
You have a rich reward, e'en here below.
May all your flock be docile to your zeal, ·
And follow in your footsteps, for their weal ;
Nor ever from that way of life depart,
Traced by a Pastor, after God's own heart!

CHAPTER V.

THE GUESTS OF THE URSULINES.

1755.

If the woes of our friends become, by sympathy, our own, it must not be deemed foreign to our subject to introduce here a brief account of the destruction of the Hôtel-Dieu, in 1755.

It was only three years since a similar · disaster had befallen the Convent and Hospital of the Ursulines of Three Rivers, as we have elsewhere related. Now it was the oldest of the Charitable Institutions in the country that was to be destroyed.

It was about mid-day, on the 7th of June that a fire, which must have been creeping on unobserved for hours, suddenly declared itself by bursting through the roof. A strong wind from the northwest fanned the flames to a tremendous conflagration. In the space of a few hours,

the Convent, the Church, the Hospital,
and out-houses, were swept away, with
all the movables, the comforts and resources, which more than a hundred years
had brought together, for the accommodation of the poor · patients, or the Community.

It is needless to say how quickly the
whole city, in alarm, was gathered to
witness the heart-rending scene;—and to
deplore the impotency of human efforts
to arrest the progress of the fiery torrent.
The whole neighbourhood was in imminent danger.

The terror of the nuns, their exertions,
their heroic courage, shared by their
friends of every grade, while removing
to a place of safety, decrepit old people,
idiots, the sick, and the maimed ; their
laudable endeavors to save from the
wreck whatever was most prized or most
needful;—all this may be imagined. But,
alas! other scenes were witnessed there,
upon which we would willingly forbid
our imagination to dwell. In this hour

of anguish, the nuns knew that one of
their beloved Sisters was at the point of
death. Must they disturb the tranquillity
of her last moments, and hasten, perhaps,
her end, by transporting the poor sufferer from her dying bed in the Infirmary, into the crowded court-yard ?
There was no other alternative, even had
there been time for deliberation.........

Another, surrounded in her cell by the
fire, seeks to descend from the fourth
story ; a ladder had been sent up to her
aid, the vigorous arms of the soldiery
holding it firm. Suddenly, while every
one shudders to behold the peril, a by-
stander shouts to her :—several steps are
missing below her feet! How the good
Angels were invoked ! and how they
aided the good Sister to preserve her
presence of mind. Seizing the two side-
pieces of the ladder, she supports herself
by her hands till she again has foot-
hold :—and thus, amid the cheers of the
crowd, she reaches the ground, narrowly
escaping however, being enveloped by

the smoke and flames, pouring now, from the lowest windows.

At last, she is safe ! But where is that other Sister, who has been seen a moment at a window, in the act of throwing out a parcel, and now has disappeared ? In vain are the frantic shouts of those who would be her deliverers ; in vain the search in every direction for some trace of the missing one ; in vain the tears and lamentations of her Sisters when, assembled at last, they find their number incomplete. Sister Anne La Joue of the Sacred Heart had perished......But it was under the eye of Him to whom she had vowed her existence. Doubtless the Lord had inspired her to make the heroic sacrifice of her life, by a perfect resignation in that terrible moment when she found herself wrapt as in a winding-sheet of flame.

Our Ursulines, from their monastery, could witness the conflagration ; they had watched with pity and dismay, the progress of the fire, and had sent the

most pressing invitations to the *Hospitalières* to take refuge under their roof.
Messengers had already made known the
melancholy details we have just given,
and the sinking flames seemed invested
with a sad and lurid glare ;—a funereal
hue that told of death.

At last the dear Nuns, now forty-nine
in number, directed their mournful steps
towards the centre of the town. Weep-
ing friends and relatives attended them
on their way, and crowds of people followed to testify their sympathy and their
affliction.........

We shall not attempt to describe the
meeting of the two Communities, few of
whom were strangers, while many were
relatives, class-mates, or remembered each
other in the capacity of former teachers
and pupils.

Rev. Mother Mailloux of St. Andrew,
the dying nun of whom we have spoken,
was tenderly borne to the Infirmary, and
cared for, according to her need. She
lived till the Monday following, expe-

riencing, in her last moments, the consolation of feeling herself passing secure
from the embrace of fraternal charity to
the bosom of the God of charity.

'The burial service and the accustomed
suffrages for the departed, were performed by both Communities, and the dear
remains of the *Hospitalière* deposited in
the vault where the deceased Ursulines
repose :—" In order, says the Annalist, that
her ashes mingling with ours may serve
to render enduring that union which has
ever subsisted between us."

The generous hospitality which, in
former days, (1651 and 1686) the Ursulines
had received at the Hôtel-Dieu, had not
been forgotten; and they esteemed themselves happy in being able to afford a return :—but, not all the ingenious devices
of friendship, not all the sympathy and
affection with which they sought to cheer
their guests, could induce these devoted
nurses of the sick to forget their precious
charge. A temporary hospital was provided, by the paternal solicitude of Bishop

de Pontbriand, the kind Jesuit Fathers having cheerfully offered, for this end, several spacious apartments of their College. Thus, at the end of three weeks, on the 28th of June, the Ursulines and their guests bade each other a tender-adieu ; — mingled emotions sent their signals to the cheek and eye, as the Spouses of Jesus separated, with those words that imply the conviction of its being a last farewell : " MAY WE MEET IN HEAVEN ! "

CHAPTER VI.

PRELUDES OF THE GREAT CRISIS.

1754—1758.

For nearly a half-century all has been in peace along the borders of the St. Lawrence. The last fifteen years, over which we have just glanced, have been as prolific of comforts in the happy homes of New France, as the next decade will be of disaster, alarm, and suffering. Troubles were now commencing along the distant frontier, and soldiers were wanted to guard the outposts of this great French empire, threatened by the Anglo-American Colonies, already strong enough to think of war and conquest.

Our Ursuline Mothers could not be indifferent, when the welfare of the country was interested. The ties of nature as well as of grace, linked them with the whole population ; and the tidings that sent grief or mourning to any hearth in town or hamlet, ever found an echo in their hearts.

The Annalist of the time, Mother de Muy of St. Helen, has left us minute details of that long campaign, the Seven Years' War, from the first bloody conflict on the shores of the Monongahela, to the day when the British trumpet of war resounded from the cliffs of Cape Diamond.

From year to year the sufferings of the people were on the increase. Now it was the failure of crops, the absence of laborers having left the land untilled ; now it was the loss of vessels, going from or to the Colony. In the course of a few months—this was in 1758—more than three hundred French merchant-ships were captured by the British Marine, with the loss of provisions, merchandise, and military stores, destined for Canada, where they were sorely needed. To these causes of distress, was added the inclemency of the seasons.

Of the month of June, 1758, we read : " The cold is so extreme that we have to kindle fires as in winter. Nothing is growing ; the flowers of the fruit-trees have been blighted by the frost ; and what is worse, the wheat-fields are frozen. There is every prospect that the harvest will be ruined. The hand of the Almighty weighs heavily upon this poor country. The English goad us, on every side ; and the Indians, won by their presents, threaten to abandon us......... We

have experienced, however, the goodness
of Divine Providence in our greatest
need. The people had passed the winter
on rations of four ounces of bread daily,
and were on the point of being reduced
to two ounces. There were no vegetables to be had, and meat was excessively
scarce.—In short, starvation was staring
us in the face, when, on the 27th of May,
a French merchant-vessel was descried
in the distance. The joy was so great
that people climbed to the roofs of their
houses, and mounted the chimney tops,
to assure themselves that the good news
was true, and to announce it to the crowds
in the streets. Greater still were the
rejoicings, when other ships were seen
coming in. At six o'clock in the evening
there were ten vessels, and a few days
later, fourteen were anchored in the late
vacant harbor.

"But the vessels have brought us sad
news of the state of religion in Europe...
and of the great efforts the English are
making to take Canada." A little later,
the writer records the taking of Louis-

burg. By the loss of that stronghold, the French colonists, still more isolated from France, were left without other resource than that energy inspired by the love of their country and their religion. It is not astonishing if Frenchmen, and Catholics viewed with horror the possibility of falling under English rule. Catholicity, was at that time, by the legislation of England, a crime. The *penal* laws were in their full force. The deplorable fate of the Acadians, was the most recent proof how ready the conqueror ever is to exclaim : " Woe to the vanquished ! "

A whole people torn from their homes, separated from each other, forced on board ships, to be borne off and cast, unprovided for, upon various inhospitable shores, for no other cause but their religion, was a terrible warning. Death seemed preferable to the misfortune of being conquered : so it was understood by the brave Montcalm and his brother-Officers, who had resolved to bury themselves under the ruins of the Colony, rather than to give it up to the enemy : so it was understood by the Colonists at large, through-out the country.

Meanwhile, the tide of misfortune that had set in against the French in America, was ever growing stronger. The last gleam of hope seemed extinguished,when the intrepid envoy who (1758–59) had penetrated, as it were, through the enemy's lines, in order to reclaim the assistance of the French Monarch, returned only to announce that his petition was rejected.

Henceforth the Colony knew itself abandoned by the mother-country, and gathering courage from the greatness of the emergency, the population rose in a mass to defend, to the last, their altars and their habitations. The dreary winter of 1758–1759, was the fourth, during which the sufferings of famine had weighed upon the whole country. The nuns who record the fact, state that they were reduced to rations with the rest, bewailing the necessity that obliged them to present, even to those who were

sick, "bread as black as their robes." They
mention that some poor Acadians, escaping the lot of their countrymen, had
wandered through the woods and wilds
till they reached Quebec, where their
sorrows and sufferings added new terrors
to the approach of the common foe.

The snows of wintry fields, at last, had
melted; the ice-bound streams were free.
Nature, refusing to assort her colors to
the sombre hues of the political horizon,
had clothed once more the earth in green,
and decked the forests with budding
leaves and fragrant blossoms. The great,
glorious River, spreading out its broad
expanse to the warm sun of early summer,
seemed to ask news of the many welcome
ships that were wont, at this season, to
mirror their white sails on its bosom.

Suddenly, on the 26th of June, the
British war-fleet, stood in sight. It was
a formidable array of armed vessels, including twenty-two ships of the line, forty
frigates and transports, bearing 30,000
soldiers and seamen, flushed with the

recent victories that had rendered thei masters of the Gulf, and elated with the good fortune that had given them a prosperous voyage. Our Annalist could not have known their strength, but her words were a prophecy when she exclaimed : " The country is lost ! "

CHAPTER VII.

DURING THE SIEGE.

1759.

It had not required the electric wires to carry from one end of the country to the other the news that a formidable English fleet was on its way to attack the capital of Canada. The gigantic preparations for this final invasion were known, but instead of giving way to despondency, the entire population were animated with courage in proportion to the danger. A

levy of militia included every male capable of bearing arms, between the ages of
fifteen and sixty. Old men of seventy
and boys of thirteen or fourteen, tendered
their services, and would not be refused.
The citizens of Quebec, after sending their
families to a place of safety, were needed
to strengthen the garrison, and to man
the batteries that commanded the harbor.
All along the shores of the St. Lawrence,
the defenceless population that remained
in hamlet or village—the infirm and aged,
the women and children, under the care
of their priest and the civil officers, had
orders to retire from their houses as the
fleet approached, hiding themselves with
their effects in the woods at the base of
the mountains, or in the wild forests of
the southern plains.

 . The army under Montcalm, made up
of five battalions of regulars, wasted and
worn with hard service and poor fare, had
been augmented by about 6000 Canadians,
who had not suffered less from famine
and hardships; but who felt themselves
invincible in their ardor to defend their

homes, their country and their religion. From their cloister, the Ursulines could see the disposition of the army, its centre at Beauport, its wings, extending from the bridge of boats on the St. Charles to the battery on the rugged cliffs of the Montmorency.

On the first of July, the English fleet had reached the Island of Orleans, whence the inhabitants had just fled to the appointed place of concealment : the men-of-war lay at anchor, and the troops disembarking, set foot on the soil they had been sent to conquer for the English crown.

Cautiously they continued to sound their way, as they entered the magnificent harbor, capable of containing four hundred vessels as proud as theirs. But they were not suffered to proceed unmolested. On every side the French were alert, and the cannons of the garrison were not idle.

On the 12th of July, at nine in the evening, from batteries erected at Point Levy, the enemy began a heavy cannonade on the city. The Lower-Town, at only a mile's distance from the opposite shore, had been deserted by its inhabitants, who foresaw its coming fate. The red-hot balls and bomb shells did their work of destruction, shattering many houses and setting them on fire. The Upper Town, which had not been so completely evacuated, proved to be within the range of the enemy's guns, and the greatest panic prevailed. Our Mothers, ever willing to hope for the best, had not abandoned the cloister. "But, says the Annalist, at the first discharge from the English batteries, the Convent was struck in many places. We passed the night before the Blessed Sacrament, in such terrors as may be imagined."

With the return of day-light, it was resolved to remove the Community to a place of greater safety. It would have been temerity to remain longer within reach of the murderous projectiles which had done such execution in a single night. The venerable Superioress, Mother Migeon of the Nativity, who had provided herself

with a *permission* in case of such an emergency, invites each one to make up her
little parcel,—such as she can carry—and
to follow her, while there is a pause in the
firing. But suddenly, there is a little
delay. No! the Convent will not be
totally abandoned. Ten of the Sisters,
with the *Depositaire*, Mother Davanne of
St. Louis de Gonzague at their head, have
offered to remain ; the Chaplain, Rev. Mr.
Resche, with two of his friends, have
volunteered to be their guardians; and
all are satisfied with the arrangement.
Mother Superior gives her blessing to the
little band as they sorrowfully bid each
other adieu. Some among those who
were going forth from their peaceful
cloister, were very aged; others were weak
and sickly. Did any then foresee that, for
two of those beloved Mothers, it was a last
adieu as they issued sorrowful and trembling from their Convent-home?

They pass down the street through
Palace-Gate. They give no thought to
the splendors of the Intendant Bigot's
Palace, which they pass; nor to his iniqui-

tous proceedings, of which they were probably uninformed:—but hurry on, by the nearest paths, across the meadows that intervene between the town and the General Hospital; for that is the asylum they are seeking, adding their numbers to the hundreds of defenceless wanderers already sheltered by those benevolent ladies.

The General Hospital had became a " city of refuge " for nearly 800 persons. The nuns of the Hôtel-Dieu were already there, and like the Ursulines, were prepared to take their share of the fatigues, devolving upon the *Hospitalières*. Every apartment was crowded. All the out-houses, the sheds, and barns, were occupied : every garret and empty corner was filled with the wretched pallets of the poor refugees, their bundles of clothing, and whatever they valued or sought to preserve. It was among these sorrowing people, whose countenances betrayed anxiety and consternation, that the good Bishop de Pontbriand, who had taken refuge at Charlesbourg, was seen every day, coming like an angel of consolation, to comfort, encourage and bless.

Later, as numbers of the wounded were brought in, the church was transformed into a hospital. The only place that remained vacant was the nuns' choir, where the poor people crowded to assist daily at the Holy Sacrifice of the Mass. Th're, also, the three Communities assemble l to recite the Divine Office, the only respite they allowed themselves from their labors in assisting the poor and needy, or tending the sick. Thus passed the long summer; for long and tedious it seemed to those whose aching hearts were swayed by alternate hope and dread. Each day brought some new cause for mourning, or some new spectacle of woe. Fires, kindled by the red-hot projectiles, continued the work of devastation. At times, it seemed as if the whole city was doomed to perish, in one vast conflagration. If the garrison, within their stronghold and battling with the enemy, were safe, it was not thus with the few inhabitants

who still ventured to traverse the streets,
or who persisted in remaining within
their own dwellings. News of fatal accidents, occurring almost daily, increased
the anxiety of the absent nuns for their
brave Sisters, left at *home*. How often
their eyes were turned to that dear spot!
What anguish they endured as from time
to time they discovered, or got tidings of
some new devastation. One day the red-
hot balls falling upon a shed, set it on fire:
all the out-houses of the Convent were
consumed, the flames rising high and
threatening to extend to all the buildings around. Another time they witnessed the burning of the Cathedral and
all the dwelling-houses in its vicinity. A
heart-rending thing for all, was the devastation perpetrated along the shores of the
St. Lawrence, where houses and churches
were wantonly set on fire, and depreda-
tions of every kind committed.

We need not ask if the poor exiles often
fled to the foot of the Tabernacle to find
strength and hope, — meekly accepting
the bitter chalice from the hand of God,

and saying with the patient man of old :
" Though He slay me yet will I trust in
Him."

At length, it was September. That
month, so short in Canada, with its balmy
atmosphere, its lustrous skies, its pleasant
harvest scenes, had brought them the
Feast of the Virgin's birth-day ; and with
it, hopes of security. Evidently the English were tired of their useless efforts to
gain any advantage over the French.
The City was nearly destroyed ; but it was
not taken. They had once tried to attack Montcalm in his intrenchments on
the Beauport plains, and it had been a
failure. Would not the early autumn,
so quickly followed by winter, force the
enemy to withdraw their fleet ? For
several days the troops, which had so
long been idle, were moving in various
directions along the shores, above and
below Quebec ; but they were watched,
and all weak points were guarded. No
one knew the daring project the intrepid
Wolfe was meditating. It was a last re-

source ; if it failed, the campaign was over.

Our readers know how every thing conspired to render the enterprise successful. The silence of the night told no tales of the stealthy march of 5000 soldiers. The echoes of the cliff only brought the listening boatmen the necessary password. No rock of the shelving precipice gave way under the quick footsteps of the eager English soldier.

The first rays of the morning of that memorable 13th September, fell on the glittering arms of an enemy—not yet within the gates—but on the heights which alone had rendered the city impregnable. The "Battle of the Plains" · had taken place before noon, crowding into the brief space of one hour, events that have changed the destinies of New France : while History has kept her record, and taught the same lesson as Faith : "That all things work together for good to them that love God."

September, 1759.

How fared the General Hospital, with its many inhabitants on the day of battle? How fared the three Communities, on the morrow of that defeat of the French army, which had been accomplished almost at their very doors?

The Hospital, from the hour of midnight, has been surrounded by a detachment of those same Scotch Highlanders, whose bright claymores glittered so terribly as they pursued down the hill-side, Montcalm's routed forces. But their attitude now, is not hostile. Their commander, Capt. McDonell, has explained, in a brief interview with the three Superiors, the necessity he is under of investing the place, in order to prevent a surprise. He has pledged his word that no harm shall befall the inmates of Notre-Dame-des-Anges. He claims their bene-volent services for the wounded of the English army, who are brought in, indis-criminately with the French, from the battle-field.

Alas ! among the latter, the nuns often found their own near relations, without being able to do more to soothe their dying hour, than for the strangers, com mitted to their charity.

The remnants of the French army, after turning many times upon their pursuers, had completely disappeared. Their tents were still standing along the plains of Beauport; but their batteries and trenches were silent and solitary ; their guns, still pointed, were mute. Along the battle-field of the Plains, still reeking with gore and covered with the slain, the victors were opening the turf, to hide from view the hideous effects of war ; bearing off such of the poor victims as still survived, and hastening to intrench themselves, to secure their position, so fortunately gained.

Around the Citadel, groups of French officers are seen in consultation; their gloomy countenances tell of indecision, weariness, and despondency. Within, a feeble garrison of seven or eight hundred men, await the orders of their superior officers : the soldier's watch-word is obedience.

At nine o'clock in the evening of that 14th September, a funeral cortege, issuing from the Castle, winds its way through the dark and obstructed streets, to the little Church of the Ursulines. With the heavy tread of the coffin-bearers, keep time the measured footsteps of the military escort,—De Ramsay, and the officers of the garrison,—following to their last resting place, the lifeless remains of their illustrious Commander-in Chief. No martial pomp was displayed around that humble bier; but the hero who had afforded, at his dying hour, the sublime spectacle of a christian, yielding up his soul to God in the most admirable sentiments of faith and resignation, was not laid in unconsecrated ground.

No burial rite could be more solemn than that hurried evening service, performed by torch-light, under the dilapidated roof of a sacred asylum, where the soil had first been laid bare by one of the rude engines of war; the grave tones of the priests murmuring the *Libera me, Domine*, were responded to by the sighs and tears of consecrated virgins, henceforth the guardians of the precious deposit, which, but for, "inevitable fate" would have been reserved to honor some proud mausoleum.

With gloomy forebodings and bitter thoughts, De Ramsay and his companions in arms, withdrew in silence; nor ventured to

> " Discharge one farewell shot
> O'er the tomb where a hero was buried ! "

A few citizens had gathered in, and among the rest, one led by the hand his little daughter, [1] who, looking into the

1. Mother Dubé of St. Ignatius, who died in 1839, at the age of eighty-nine.

open grave, saw and remembered more than three-fourths of a century later, the rough wooden box, which was all the ruined city could afford to enclose the remains of her Defender !

But while all is silent again around the Convent of the Ursulines, let us transport ourselves in spirit to the Hospital, where are assembled so many poor trembling women and children ; homeless widows and orphans ; helpless old men, and sick or wounded soldiers.

Stunned with the events of the last forty-eight hours, the final result of which is yet uncertain, all await in cruel suspense. Had the last hour of the French dominion in Canada passed away ? had the Colony exchanged masters with that brief struggle, the Battle of the Plains ? Would not the French troops rally and return, awakening again the death-telling roar of artillery, and exposing to the fatal stroke even that remnant of friends and relations ?

But at this late evening hour, sleep and

sorrow have closed the eyes of all,—except those who suffer, or who watch to alleviate sufferings. Of both classes there are not a few, and among them we find our dear Ursuline Mothers. One little dormitory is all that the most tender hospitality has been able to assign them ; and to-night, it is transformed into a death-chamber for two of their number,—two whose last hour has been hastened by the calamitous scenes through which they had just passed. Mother Jeryan of St. Joseph, rescued from captivity among the Indians, and received forty years ago among the daughters of St. Ursula, will no more return to her beloved Monastery; but exiled from her second home, she has departed to her happy eternal home in heaven.

The second victim, whose heart broke —it would seem – with. the death-blow given to her country, was Mother Char-lotte de Muy of St. Helen ; the same whose hand has traced for us all the details of the war, up to the day when the nearer approach of the enemy gave her a pre-sentiment .of what would be the result of the impending crisis.

If the brave General, whose deeds she recorded with such interest, rejoiced that he was permitted to die before Quebec would surrender; the humble spouse of Christ, herself the daughter of one who had governed a part of the Colony, (Louisiana,) resigned herself all the more cheerfully to go forth from this world, that she might not see her country ruled by a foreign power.

The soldier has his grave under the roof of the Monastery; the two Ursulines repose in a little garden-cemetery, beside the Hospital where so many a brave soldier expired : their ashes mingle with those of the generous *Hospitalières*, whose friendship was to our dear Mothers the sweetest solace of their exile.

A few days later, the City had capitu-lated. The victors enter, to behold the ruins they have made; and are forced to repair them, to find lodgings for them-

selves. The Red-cross of St. George is
flying from the heights of Cape Diamond,
instead of the lily-spotted banner of St.
Louis, when the Ursulines re-enter their
cloister :—it was on the 21st of September
after an absence of seventy days.

The spectacle which the Convent presented, has been graphically depicted in
our Annals :—" The building that serves
for the Extern-school, in ruins; the sacris-
ty, the chapel of Saints, and the Church,
pierced by cannon-balls and bomb-shells;
several cells in the dormitory much damaged ; roofs broken in ; chimneys demolished ; the laundry, dilapidated .by a
bomb which had traversed the floor of
the Community......Yet, adds the writer,
with charactaristic gratitude, our losses
would have been much greater, had not
eight of our dear Sisters been courageous
enough to remain in the Convent during
the siege. Regardless of fatigue, and exposed to be wounded or killed by the
falling projectiles, they were ever on the
watch, and succeeded in saving most of
the windows, the statues, the paintings,

the two tabernacles and altar furniture, with other precious articles, which had they not been removed, would have been damaged or destroyed."

As to the aspect of the city, after a two months' siege, let our readers recall to mind the fact, that the Ursuline Convent, which they have just contemplated, was one of the edifices that had suffered the least. Six hundred houses were so riddled by shot and shell as to be tenantless, when they were not totally destroyed. The Cathedral, the Seminary, the Bishop's Palace, the Intendant's, &c. were in ruins. The residences of the Jesuits, the Recollets, and the Hôtel-Dieu, had suffered severely. In Lower-Town, but one house had escaped destruction; and blackened, crumbling walls were all that remained of that favorite church, *Notre-Dame des Victoires.*

It will not be without interest to subjoin here

THE COMMUNITY IN 1759: or *the names*

and ages of the Nuns, who witnessed the events related in the last chapters.

Rev. Mother Marie-Anne Migeon de Bransac of
    the Nativity, Superioress, aged   74
    Genevieve Boucher of S. Pierre,
    Assistant...................   83
    Marie-Louise Gaillard of the Blessed
    Virgin, Zelatrix.............   62
    Françoise de Hertel of St. Exupere   79
    Genevieve de La Grange of St. Louis   65
    Esther Wheelwright of the Infant
    Jesus   62
    Marguerite Cloutier of St. Monica.   59
    Marie-Anne de Boucherville of St.
    Ignatius.....................   63
    Marie-Anne Buteau of St. Agnes..   61
    Marie-Charlotte de Muy of St.
    Helen [1].....................   65
    Marie-Claire Gaillard of St.Thomas   57
    Mary-Dorothy Jeryan of St. Jo-
    seph [1].....................   54
    Madeleine-Genevieve Perthuis of
    St. Charles.................   58
    Anne-Catherine Petit of St. Stanis-
    laus   50
    Jeanne-Claire Marchand of St.
    Etienne.....................   40

[1] Deceased at the General Hospital, Sept. 14th.

Rev. Mother Marie-Marguerite Davanne of St.
  Louis de Gonzague............ 40
Marie Elizabeth Richard of St. Au-
  gustin 38
Marie-Catherine Lagere of St. Ga-
  briel. 40
Marie-Antoinette Poulin of St.
  Francis 36
Genevieve de Lantagnac of St.
  Henry...................... 36
Angelique de Lantagnac of St.
  Mary...................... 29
Marie-Françoise Poulin of St. An-
  thony.... 26
Marie-F. Cureux de St. Germain of
  St. Chrysostom 27
Marie-C. Lefebvre of St. Geneviève 26
Marie-Joseph DesRoches of the An-
  gels 36
Louise-Françoise Soupiran of St.
  Ursula..................... 25
Marie-Madeleine Cureux de St.
  Germain of St. Agatha 23
M.-Charlotte Brassard of St. Clare. 29
Angelique C. Parisé of St. John. 24
M.-Françoise Comparé of St. Fran-
  çois-Xavier. 22
M.-Madeleine Massot of St. Fran-
  cis of Paul 26
M.-Anne Brassard of St. Magdalen. 23

Thirteen Lay Sisters :—

Sr. Marguerite Gravel of St. Clement.........

Marie-Anne Racine of the Resurrection....

M. Julienne Maufis of St. Andrew........

Marie-Joseph Gagnon of St. Paul ....

Marie-Joseph Patenôte of St. Francis ..

Genevieve Mimaux o! the Presentation ...

Marie-Jeanne Bédard of St. Hyacinthe....

Elizabeth Le Vasseur of St. Ambrose..:....

M. Rosalie Bedard of St. Fr. Regis........

M. Angélique Toupin of St. Martha.......

M. Elizabeth Bédard of St. Denis........ .

Angélique Déry of St. Thecla ....

Louise-Gertrude Hamel of St. Anne.......

Total : forty-five.

CHAPTER IX.

PRISONERS OF WAR :

THE CONVENT BECOMES A HOSPITAL.

1759–1763.

In letters written after the return
our Mothers to their cloister, they sty
themselves—and with reason—*Prisone*

of war. They are uncertain what will be the fate of the Convent, or the Country. Will they be obliged to go to France? Will not the English lose by treaty what they have gained by conquest? Or will not the French Monarch, at last, come to succor his faithful subjects?

Our readers have seen what damages the Convent had suffered. Besides these, the farm on the St. Charles, belonging to the nuns, had been ravaged, their cattle driven off; the crops of wheat and hay were destroyed. They had no fuel for the coming winter; their stock of linen and other effects which they were accustomed to receive from France, was exhausted. They could expect no help from their friends, when the whole country was a ruin. In this conjuncture, Providence raised up protectors for them, where they could least have expected.

General Murray, entering the city as master, had promised that the Religious Communities should not be molested. He paid the Ursulines an early visit, and,

from his first interview with the aged
Superioress, seems to have conceived for
her the highest esteem. Assuring her
of his special protection for the Community, he manifested his wish to occupy a
part of the Convent as a hospital, for the
wounded or sick of the army.

The proposal was acceded to with a
good grace, and immediately, workmen
were sent in to make the necessary reparations. Commencing by the Church,
the only one in the City that was not in
ruins, they had it prepared for Divine
service, on the 24th of September. Ten
days later, the sick soldiers were brought
in, several apartments having been put
in readiness. The venerable Superioress
cheerfully accepted the duties of her new
position, and distributed her nuns through
the various departments of the new *Hospital.* Divine charity taught the nuns to
banish every other feeling but compassion from their hearts, and to wait upon
these strangers, lately their enemies, as if
they had seen in each the Divine Saviour
himself.

In the mean time the cold season was advancing. The regiment of Highlanders, quartered upon the Convent, had their share in the hard labors imposed upon all the soldiers in providing the City with fuel. Exposed by the peculiarities of their costume to suffer severely from the climate, they were objects of compassion to the good nuns, who set to work to provide substantial hose " to cover the limbs of the poor strangers." On the other hand, the convalescent officers and soldiers were eager to show their gratitude by rendering every out-door service in their power, clearing the paths around the Convent from snow, bringing as far as they were allowed, burdens of every kind, wood and water, the daily provisions which were ordered from the Commissariat, or from the baker's office. The prejudices they had previously entertained, and their opinions of a "nunnery" were soon modified, by seeing the humility and real charity with which these Religious accomplished the tasks, necessity had imposed upon them. In Rev.

Mother Migeon of the Nativity, the Superioress, whose merits and qualifications fitted her for the trying situation, and in all the Sisterhood, they beheld persons, to whom they could not refuse the tribute of the highest esteem.

As to the religious exercises of the military, during the first months of their occupation of the city, we learn from that echo of the past, tradition, that the church of the Ursulines, where the Catholic population of the city assembled for the Holy Sacrifice of the mass, was occupied at other times, for the Anglican rite.

It is easy to conceive with what secret sorrow—if a stronger word would not better express the sentiment—our Mothers yielded up their " altars and their shrines," to those who professed no respect for either. Doubtless, at such hours, if forced to leave the choir vacant, not a few took refuge in the chapel of Saints, to pray for those who honored not the Saints. Where the *Chaplain of the troops* resided, it is not said ; but the nuns' chaplain, Rev. Mr. Resche, had taken up his lodgings in the *parloir* [1] during the Siege; and he continued to occupy the apartment during those difficult times, in order to be at hand whenever his presence might be required.

If the winter was a long and painful one to the Ursulines, if some of the Sisters sank under fatigue, there were other causes of suffering, besides the labors and inconveniences to which they were exposed. They knew well that the French army had not surrendered. The brave De Levis had assembled at Montreal all the forces that remained ; determined to make one more, desperate effort to save the Country. Descending the river with the first appearance of spring, his intention was to drive the enemy from Quebec, before their returning vessels could find a passage through the ice in the Gulf. On the 28th of April, he met the English

---

[1] The same room, — the two parts being now thrown into one — is occupied at the present day by the Chaplain of the Monastery.

troops for the second battle on the **Plains.**
Alas, for good counsel on such occasions!
could the all-wise decrees of Divine Providence have been read beforehand, **how**
much blood, uselessly shed, might **have**
been spared ! But the people of **Canada**
could not believe that their country, discovered, conquered and colonised by
Frenchmen, could be given up by **France:**
and while they fought

> " For their altars and their fires,
> God, and their native land,"

with heroic courage, they never **expected**
to be left alone to cope with an enemy **so**
powerful.

　Three dreadful hours had covered the
ground with the slain. Friend and foe
lay in promiscuous heaps on that field of
the dead. The English troops had been
driven back in disorder. But of **what**
avail was this partial advantage, or the
destruction of lives and property **during**
the following five-days' Siege ?...... **Al-**
ready reinforcements for the **English**
army were at hand. The first spring

vessels were descried, sailing up the chan-
nel. If, for a moment, the intrepid De
Levis fancied that these were French
Men-of-war, hastening to his rescue, he
was soon undeceived. The Red-cross of
England was flying at the mast-head !

Frenchmen ! Canadians ! cease your
desperate strife. Overwhelmed by numbers, you may desist without shame ; for
you have nobly defended a righteous
cause. The fate of nations is in the hand
of God ; and later, when you know why
He denied you victory, you will bless his
apparent rigor and own that " He doth
all things well ! "

After that second Siege of Quebec was
over, our Annalist writes : " It was now,
more than ever, that our Convent became
a hospital; with difficulty we found means
to retain lodgings for ourselves." Hour
after hour the wounded English soldiers
were brought in. The horrid spectacle of
mangled and mutilated limbs, of blood
and gore, of acute suffering in all its
varied forms, was an appalling one for

Ursulines : but they had already seen what were the dismal effects of war, and had taken lessons in the dressing of wounds, during the great Siege ;—they found courage in their charity, and continued their compassionate cares as long as there was occasion for them.

Our Annalist—no longer Mother de Muy of St. Helen,—has been too sparing of details. We may form an idea of what has been omitted, by a few lines written at the General Hospital, after the second battle of the Plains.

" How depict, says the *Hospitalière*, the horrors we have had to see and hear, during the twenty-four hours that the transit hither lasted,—the cries of the dying and the lamentations of those interested in their fate. A strength more than human is necessary at such a time, to prevent those engaged in tending such sufferers from sinking under their task.

" After having dressed more than five hundred patients, placed on beds obtained from the King's magazines, there still re-

mained others unprovided for...... Our
barns and sheds were full of the wounded..... We had in our infirmaries seventy-
two officers, of whom thirty-three died.
The amputation of legs and arms was
going on everywhere......

" The British had taken possession of
the Hôtel-Dieu, the Ursuline Convent and
private dwelling houses, for the reception
of their wounded, *who were even in greater
number than ours.*"

Our Annals mark, summarily, the death
of several of the English soldiers, within
the Monastery. One of the Halls for the
sick had the reputation of being infected
with some pestiferous malady,—but this
did not prevent the nuns from continuing
their charitable attendance.

The community Hall had been assigned
to the Officers; beneath it, a similar apartment became the Council-chamber, where
General Murray, twice a week, assembled
his military tribunal. The Class-rooms, the
pupils' Refectory and other apartments,

were transformed into sick-wards for the soldiers. [1]

In the mean time, the table of the nuns, as well as the wants of their guests, continued to be furnished by military orders.

On the 8th of September, the capitulation of Montreal, and the subsequent evacuation of the country by the French troops—sent back to France, accompanied by a great number of persons of distinction—might well have extinguished the last ray of hope of ever being reunited to the mother-country. But not so easily fade the visions which the heart, rather than the fancy, pictures. France

[1] The precise date of the departure of the military from the Monastery is not registered : apparently, it was not later than the month of June (1760).

There is a curious document to prove that the Convents knew how to obtain redress if molested. It as an Ordinance signed by the Aid-de-Camp, Th. Mills, to the purport that "The Superiors of the Convents in the City, having complained that the Religious are prevented from taking their usual recreations in their gardens by the Officers entering the enclosure:—wherefore, it is expressly forbidden henceforward that any Officer or soldier enter there," &c.

had not yet ratified the Conquest—perhaps she never would—and meanwhile,
the farmer repairing his ruined walls and
hedges, cultivates the land ; the industrious mechanic, poorer than ever, pur-
sues his daily toil ;—avoiding, as far as
possible, all contact with the strangers,
who occupy every post of honor or emolument ; who are stationed at the gates of
the City, and at the door of every hall
of Justice ; who monopolize whatever
trade and commerce can be carried on :
and who consider themselves, in all respects — as they wish to be treated — *the
lords of the land*......

Hostilities had at last ceased, and in the
calm of so disastrous a storm, more of the
dispersed families, belonging to the City,
returned to seek their former habitations.
In many cases it was but a heap of stones
and rubbish, that marked the site of their
once happy homestead. Our Mothers,
remembering the hospitality others had
exercised towards them in the days of
their exile, made room for several families who, during the winter, filled all the

available apartments of the Monastery, and its dependencies. Among the number of persons who were thus sheltered, the Annalist has noted, that " there were several deaths of children, and people of various ages; the ground near the Externs served for their burial. The bodies were removed to the public cemetery only the following year. "

While our Ursulines were thus exercising charity, at the expense of great inconvenience to themselves, they did not forget their first and most cherished obligation : during the course of the winter (1761-2) they began to take boarders, and to open a class of instruction for day-scholars. In the month of April, a certain number of children being found sufficiently prepared, the great act of the First Communion took place, under the direction of the indefatigable pastor, Rev. M. Recher.

On the same page we find another memorandum, which is a silent, but eloquent comment upon the poverty of the

Convent : " In the month of June of this present year, we received in alms from Mr. Montgolfier,[1] Superior of the Seminary of St. Sulpice, at Montreal, forty bushels of wheat, which has enabled us to sow our land on the River St. Charles. We have thus hopes of raising a little grain, since the war has not robbed us of our farm."

A little further on, we read of the loss of a vessel, on board of which were a number of Canadian families, going to France. " Only six persons were saved. This shipwreck has carried affliction and mourning into nearly every family in the country. " This was the ill-fated Augusta, where one hundred and fourteen persons, among whom, more than twenty Officers of the French nobility with their families, perished on the rocky and inhospitable coast of Cape Breton.

If the arms of England were fully

---

[1] Mr. Montgolfier was charged with the ecclesiastical affairs of the diocese, and was the presumptive candidate for the vacant See of Quebec.

triumphant in the New World, if nearly all North America owned her sway, now that the French possessions had become hers, the "Seven years' War" had not yet come to a conclusion in Europe. This unsettled state of affairs beyond the Atlantic, was watched with intense interest by the brave and loyal Canadian Frenchmen, who had been compelled to lay down their arms—but not their hopes! It was only with the news of the Treaty that ratified the conquest, in 1763, that the final act of acceptation was made; and with it another more hearty act of thanksgiving, on being assured that the rights of Religion would be respected. In Quebec, the public expression of gratitude "for the blessing of peace and the continuation of the Catholic Religion," was ordained, and on the 24th of June a solemn *Te Deum* was chanted in the Church of the Ursulines.

That the hope of a return to the French government was only given up at the last moment, appears in all the correspondence of the period. Thus, after the Treaty, one of our nuns, writing to our Parisian Ursulines, says : "I know how sincerely you have shared the afflictions that have weighed upon us for several years past. A treaty of peace, so long desired, but concluded on terms so contrary to our hopes, has filled up the measure of our sorrows. We have felt the disappointment the more sensibly, from having flattered ourselves so long that the final arrangements would be very different, for we could not persuade ourselves that Canada would be so easily given up. Nothing is left for us but to adore with submission the impenetrable decrees of the Almighty." The annals are more reserved in their comments : they write for posterity and prudently leave all things to be decided by experience. We find merely the following note : " On the 24th of May, 1863, a Treaty of Peace was signed between the king of France and of England. Canada remains to the English. God grant that Religion may ever continue to flourish!"

CHAPTER X.

OTHER TRIALS AND CONSOLATIONS:

BISHOP BRIAND; THE BOARDING-SCHOOL RE-OPENED.

1760—1775.

One of the most afflicting dispensations of Divine Providence, in a religious point of view, at this epoch, was the decease of Bishop de Pontbriand ; this occurred at Montreal, on the 8th of June, 1760 [1].

[1] It was not as a mere figure of Rhetoric that the Sacred Orator exclaimed :—

" Pleurez, infortunée Colonie, pleurez, parce que, le pasteur frappé, vous avez tout lieu de craindre de voir bientôt le troupeau dispersé, et d'être comme des brebis errantes, sans pasteur et sans guide, exposées à la fureur des loups. Pleurez, terres fécondes en fruits de grâces et de salut; pleurez, dans la crainte de voir bientôt le froment des élus, ravagé par les incursions des méchants, ou étouffé par l'ivraie que l'homme ennemi y fera croître en abondance."

Oraison funèbre, prononcée à Montréal le 25 sept., 1760, par M. Jolivet.

Since the arrival of the eminent Prelate
in Canada (1741), he had proved himself
in every way, the good Pastor, the friend,
and benefactor, the father of his people.
After the events of .the 13th September,
(1759) he had followed the French army
to Montreal, continuing to sacrifice the
remnant of his patrimony, for the relief of
the indigent; his health, in the discharge
of his pastoral duties, in cares and solicitude of every kind ; advising, exhorting
and encouraging, the defenders of Canada,
in a cause deemed identical with that of
Religion. Could he have terminated
more gloriously his career, than by laying
down his life, with the last ray of hope
for the triumph of that Cause ?

On the other hand, what a critical moment for the Church of Canada to be
deprived of her Pastor ! The ranks of the
clergy, already weakened by numerous
deaths within the past six or seven years,
required to be filled by new ordinations;
—but the consecrating hand was still and
cold. Religious Communities, so dependent on Episcopal authority, shared the

public anxiety, — and redoubled their prayers. It was not without good reason, for nothing was farther from the will of the new government than to give the deceased Prelate a successor.

Our Ursulines had other trials within their own enclosure.

The Community had been severely visited by mortality, during that period of alarm and war we have just traversed. It is not without emotion we read of two good lay Sisters, whose death, in the spring of 1760, is attributed to over-exertion during the winter, in taking care of the sick soldiers.

There had been fifteen deaths, and but nine professions, from 1753 to 1763. The last novice admitted before the Conquest, had pronounced her vows in 1758. From that time, the novitiate welcomed no other candidate, and finally remained vacant. Uncertain of their own fate, prudence forbade the nuns to admit any new member, to share the possible eventualities in store for themselves ; on the other hand, in the untried difficulties which, with the

English flag, had settled like an impenetrable and gloomy mist upon all the face
of the Country, what tender father and
mother but would have gathered nearer
their bosom, and held in a closer embrace
the beloved objects of parental solicitude ?

It was only in 1766, that the door of
the novitiate was re-opened. It belonged,
certainly, to the special Protector of the
Convent to lead the way ; accordingly it
was on the eve of his Feast, the 19th of
March, that Miss Catherine Besançon,
daughter of a respectable merchant of
Quebec, received, after her three months'
probation, the white veil, with the name
of St. Joseph. She was soon joined by
two other young ladies, Miss Marie
Joseph Blais of the Parish of St. Pierre,
River du Sud,) and Miss Louise Taschereau, daughter of the Hon. Th. Taschereau, member of the Supreme Council
of Quebec, Treasurer of the Marine &c.
Miss Taschereau, known in religion as
Mother St. Francis-Xavier, was destined
to long and useful years, as we shall have
occasion to note.

If the losses and damages the Convent had incurred during the war, had reduced the nuns to great poverty, this was notably aggravated by other causes which affected the Country at large. By the change of government in Canada, all the paper-money in circulation had become useless ; while property owned in France, was suddenly reduced to one fourth of its value, with a further discount upon the interest, even, of this fraction.

To add to the difficulty, all commerce with France was prohibited ; yet what credit or facility for business-transactions, could the Canadian merchant, if not already ruined, hope for in London ? On the other hand, how many articles of the first necessity, especially for the church and altar, or for the apparel of persons living in religious houses, so long proscribed in England, were no longer to be found on the list of English manufactures ? [1]

[1] During many years, it was impossible for our nuns to procure a supply of that fine fabric for veils which the French called *étamine*, but for which the English had neither name nor equivalent.

Obliged by the state of penury to which they were reduced, to seek some means of subsistence, our Mothers had recourse especially, to a delicate species of embroidery, technically called *bark-work*. This pretty, and novel species of " painting with the needle " in which dyed moose-hair replaces the usual shades of silk, and the soft, leather-like outer-bark of the white-birch-tree, is used instead of the rich tissues of brocade or velvet, was much admired and sought for by English ladies and gentlemen, — who had not come over to Canada with empty purses.

At a later date, gilding for the decoration of churches, tabernacles, &c., is mentioned as bringing in a small profit, whereby to avoid contracting debts, of which our Mothers appear to have ever had a just horror.

An event which served to revive the hopes of the faithful, and rejoice all who had the true interests of the Colony at heart, was the nomination of Rev. John-Olivier Briand, V. G., as Bishop of Quebec.

This important concession in favor of the Catholic Church, although implied in the Articles of the Capitulation, had not been obtained from the royal will in England without difficulty and delay. The arrival of the eminent Prelate in June, 1766, was hailed with joy, proportionate to the anxiety with which the religious population of Canada had watched the long deliberations that had retarded his consecration.

In the new Bishop, the Community welcomed an ancient Superior, and a devoted Friend ; his new title and powers had only rendered him doubly paternal. The dilapidated cloister-walls, the Extern school-house, and many other parts of the Monastery, which the poverty of the nuns had not allowed them to repair since the Siege, quickly drew the attention of the compassionate Prelate. With as much delicacy as generosity, he no sooner discovered their wants than he employed himself to relieve them. Often the first intimation of the proposed reparation, would be the sight of workmen,

busy with their tools around the ruins.
Like a good father, he loved to soothe and
cheer his daughters in Christ; he de-
lighted to appear at their pious festivals,
giving them the pontifical Mass, or
presiding, crosier in hand, at the ceremonies of Taking the Veil, or making
Profession. In a word, he availed himself of every opportunity for promoting
the welfare, temporal and spiritual, of the
Community.

At the conclusion of Bishop Briand's
first Episcopal visit of the Monastery, a
duty of his charge, the Annalist makes
the following record :—

"Our illustrious Prelate has just concluded the visitation of our Monastery,
in which he proceeded with the greatest
charity and to our entire satisfaction.

"His exhortation, at the close, was so
consoling and so full of encouragement,
that our hearts were filled with new zeal
for our own perfection and for the glory
of God. Notwithstanding the poverty
and miseries of every kind, occasioned by

the war, our good Bishop found the Community full of piety, and as regular as
ever, so he assured us ;—wishing us a
thousand blessings with the grace to preserve, in this house, to the end of time,
the spirit of our first Foundresses. God
grant that it may be so ! "

Another great consolation was reserved
for the Ursulines, at this period, in the beatification of the Foundress of the Order,
St. Angela.

The happy event was celebrated with
as much of the outward demonstrations
of joy as if the whole country had still
been Catholic ; there was only wanting
in the midst of the pious assembly the
éclat that would formerly have been
afforded by the presence of a Governor,
and his brilliant retinue. In place of this,
the Nuns record the joy and devotion
with which crowds of people came
to implore the protection of the newly-
crowned Servant of God ; remarking that
several persons of distinction, diseased or
infirm, caused themselves to be trans-

ported to our Church, in order to manifest openly their confidence in her intercession.

But the consolation chiefly prized by these Ursulines, so worthy of their name, was the facility they had found in pursuing unmolested the principal exercice of their vocation, the Instruction of Youth.

We have seen already, that no sooner had the Monastery ceased to serve as a hospital than there were found other occupants of the recent sick-wards. "All the winter, says the Annalist, in the spring of 1761, we have had a certain number of Boarders, and as many Day-Scholars as we could accommodate."

The lists of the former show thirty-seven Boarders, among whom English names begin already to appear.

The number of new scholars inscribed during the following year, would indicate about fifty pupils. The Annals dispel all doubt on the subject by the following summary remarks in 1775 :

" It has been a great consolation for us, in the midst of so many difficulties and trials, to see our Classes always well filled, there being often as many as sixty boarders, French and English. The latter are naturally very gentle and docile : but it is sad not to be allowed to bring them up in our holy Faith. The Day-Scholars are numerous, and would be more so, if we had more nuns to teach them."

To some of our readers, these lines, written with the usual brevity and candor of our Convent Record, have been suggestive; and they demand of themselves, what is to be thought of the accusations so often heard against Catholic populations, their ignorance, want of enterprise, &c., &c.

Really, it does not appear as if the Canadians of old, any more than those of present times, were indifferent to the value of education. The City, made desolate by a cruel war; almost every house in ruins; the fruit of many years of labor and economy, for ever gone ; commerce

annihilated, and every avenue to wealth
or emolument obstructed;—yet, hardly
has the soldier returned to his ruined
homestead, and assembled the scattered
members of his household, than he en-
quires, who are those that have not been
instructed for their first Communion ; how
many cannot read and write : he examines
if these can possibly be spared from home,
and straightway they are despatched to
school.

Honor then to them, to whom honor is
due ! These French Canadians, we know,
manifested more solicitude for the main-
tenance of their religion and the security
of their religious Institutions than for any
mere temporal interest ; their attitude
during all this trying crisis, being such
as to elicit the admiration and sympathy
of the English Governors themselves,
when they were men of liberal views and
of real merit.

In fact, it soon began to be apparent to
the thoughtful observers of the times,
that the Conquest of Canada had been

permitted by Divine Providence, for the greater safety and protection of its inhabitants. A letter written by one of our nuns—Mother Marchand of St. Etienne—as early as 1767, will serve to elucidate this point. It is addressed to the Ursulines of Paris, as follows : —

" The news we have had from France this year, as far as regards religion, grieves us profoundly. Although expatriated by the fate of war, our hearts are as French as ever, and this makes us doubly sensible to the decline of that dear Country. I cannot help saying it is as well to be in Canada, where we enjoy the greatest tranquillity. We are not in the least molested on the score of religion. We have a Governor who, by his moderation and benignity, is the delight of every one, and a Bishop who is the joy and consolation of his flock. If money were not so scarce, and every thing so dear, we should have nothing to desire." At a later date, Mother St Louis de Gonzague writes : " Religion is perfectly free

at present ; if any depart from their duty,
it is their own fault. People say that it
is not the same in Paris, where religious
Communities suffer a sort of persecution ;
we are told that even you were obliged
to make a secret of your festival, celebrating the beatification of our Blessed
Mother Angela. We have no such difficulty under the government of the English."

CHAPTER XI.

REV. MOTHER MARIE-ANNE MIGEON OF THE NATIVITY,

AND OTHER SUPERIORS DURING 25 YEARS.

The services which Rev. Mother Migeon of the Nativity rendered her Monastery, were not merely of that deep and
silent kind, afforded by the edifying life
of every good Religious. Placed at the

head of the Community in 1735, she became conspicuous for those qualities most
desirable in a Superior; and thus drew
repeatedly upon herself—with the confidence and affection of her Sisters—the
burden of authority. But twice during a
full quarter of a century [1735–1760], and
that for a space of three years only was
this beloved Mother allowed a respite
from the cares of government :—it was
observing the *Constitutions* to the letter.

Let us pause a while, dear Reader, in
the company of one, who merited so large
a share in the hearts of her contemporaries, and who challenges still the admiration and gratitude of the Virgins of the
cloister.

Born in Ville-Marie in 1685, Marie-Anne
was the youngest child of J. B. Migeon de
Branzac, Lieutenant General of Montreal.
Her mother, Catherine Gaucher de Belle-
ville, was one of those truly Christian
women, whose example is a more powerful incentive to virtue, for all who depend

upon her, than would be the most eloquent exhortations. It was only at the
approach of the period for that great act
of a Christian life, the First Communion,
that Mrs. Migeon prepared to resign her
tender charge into the hands of the Ursulines; and sent her daughter to Quebec
to continue an education commenced on
so firm a basis in the parental mansion.

In our classes Miss Migeon corresponded with alacrity to the care of her
worthy teachers, and completed, success-
fully, in the space of a little less than four
years, the course of studies then taught.
Returning to the bosom of her family,
the young lady, " in beauty's prime,"
richly endowed with those graces and
accomplishments the world is sure to
prize, soon had enough of its fulsome admiration to have disturbed a mind less
poised by solid judgment and sincere
piety. But " the figure of this world
which passeth away," whose delusive
light so strangely bewilders some young
ladies, dazzled not the eyes of this faithful child of Mary : she was not led away

by the siren voice of pleasure and fashion. Sweeter accents had already struck her ear, and, obeying the call of Jesus, she sought again the shades of the cloister, ambitious only to please Him whom she had chosen as the object of her affections; and willing to spend her life in imparting to youth the benefits of a Christian education, which she felt to be a treasure above all price.

On the 8th of September, 1722, just turned of seventeen, Miss Migeon de Branzac received the white veil, at the hands of Reverend J. de la Colombière, V. G of the diocese, exchanging a name, honorable in the world, for that of a Festival in which the whole world may well rejoice,—the Nativity of Mary. Two years later, she pronounced her final vows with angelic fervor.

One of the first offices confided to the pious Mother of the Nativity, was that of mistress of the Boarders. So great a responsibility seemed overwhelming to our fervent novice, who felt alarmed in proportion to the humble opinion she had of her own abilities. Her eagerness to obtain the aid of Heaven, and her diffidence of self, led her to solicit the prayers and advice of Reverend J. de la Colombière. His reply, which she ever carefully preserved, we here subjoin, as embodying the duties of an Ursuline of the present day, as well as it did of those who lived one hundred and fifty years ago.

"Your new employment, my dear Sister, demands patience and an ever ardent desire of promoting the salvation of souls. It affords you frequent opportunities of impressing upon the minds of your youthful charge, the nature of the obligations they have contracted in baptism, and of inspiring them with contempt for the pomps and vanities of the world. In a word, all the young girls under your care, should strive to become, by their piety, the living images of the most holy Virgin Mary ; they should be actuated by a noble emulation to acquire the virtues of the Queen of Angels.

Adieu ; love the Blessed Virgin and lay deep in your own heart, the foundation of every virtue as you are aware you must aim at perfection. in

order to merit the glory and happiness of being
ranked for ever among the true children of
Mary. Ever yours &c.

JOS. DE LA COLOMBIÈRE."

The office of Mistress of Class was a
light one, however, in comparison to that
of Superior, which awaited Mother Mary
of the Nativity, for the first time in 1785.
Called repeatedly, as we have already said
to the post of responsibility, she had celebrated her fiftieth year of religious profession, when came the trials and sufferings
of that memorable year of the great Siege
(1759-1760.) Yet how calm, how full of
energy, how strong by her trust in divine
Providence, how capable of counselling,
directing, and encouraging, appears this
venerable Mother! How attractive her
humility and benevolence! what delicate
propriety marked all her demeanor! That
nameless charm, with which the life-long
practice of virtue invests its possessor,
was heightened perhaps, by the vivacity
and wit peculiar to her nation, and set
off by the polish due to the usage of the
best society. To all these causes, but

above all to the merciful designs of Providence, must be attributed the influence she exerted over strangers and *Englishmen*; she, a Frenchwoman, who not only professed that Religion, hated and proscribed by their nation, but who was at the head of an Establishment, the very name of which would—at that day— have raised a cry of horror in England.

So remarkable was her success in this trying crisis, in conciliating the good will of the Officers of his British Majesty, [1] yet preserving the rights and property of the Convent, that the Bishop thought himself justified in authorising an. exception to the Rules—an exception unique in our Annals. This was to prolong the term of her government beyond the appointed time for the elections, in order to avoid any change, while as yet so many interests were at stake. To this measure there was found, it seems, one

[1] For a proof of the truly amicable relations that had sprung up between the Convent and the new government, see note B in Appendix.

dissenting voice ;—but it only served to justify the nomination, for it was that of the humble and venerable Superior herself, trembling for the consequence of one deviation from the regular discipline of the Convent.

At the age of four-score years, and more, Reverend Mother Mary of the Nativity was still a pillar of regular observance ; her pen was still as fluent, if not as elegant, as it had been thirty years previous; her intellect was as vigorous, and her piety ever more childlike and beautiful. It was only at the age of eighty-five that her strength began to fail her to such a degree, that she became, for the last eighteen months of her life, quite infirm and helpless. Yet, even to the last, the bright spirit flagged not ; the lamp, borne in the Wise Virgin's hands, was well replenished, and burned brightly, giving out vivid rays of faith, confidence, love, and desire, at the welcome approach of the Bridegroom. Pure had been the dawn, and sweet was the close of that long and useful life.

Rev. Mother La Grange of St. Louis.—This worthy Mother governed the Community from 1741 to 1744: she died in 1776, at the age of eighty-three, having borne "the sweet yoke of the Lord" in Religion, from the tender age of fifteen.

On comparing dates, we are reminded that Mother St Louis and Mother Mary of the Nativity, were pupils of Mothers Charlotte Barré of St. Ignatius, Mothers Bourdon of St. Joseph and St. Agnes ; that she lived many years with all those saintly souls, formed to the practice of perfection by Ven. Mother Marie de l'Incarnation.

Mother St. Louis is depicted as "gentle and kind, amiable in conversation, active and laborious, ready to oblige and render service, ingenious in finding time to aid the others, without neglecting the duties of her own office." Her biographer tells us of her "fervor, her regularity, her confidence in Divine Providence," enumerating the services she rendered the Community, and closes her tribute of affection in those words : " The memory of this venerable Mother will ever be most dear to us."

REV. MOTHER BOUCHER DE SAINT-PIERRE.—In seeing the advanced age of several of the Superiors of the Convent when first elected, or the late period they are continued in office, one might easily infer the great consideration the *ancients* enjoy in the Monastery. In the present instance, we have Reverend Mother St. Pierre, after occupying the second or the third rank, a full quarter of a century, called to the Superiority at the age of seventy-four. Our readers have seen elsewhere that this worthy Religious has not been forgotten in the pages of the Glimpses.

CHAPTER XII.

THE CONVENT DURING THE SIEGE OF 1775.

DIFFICULTIES OF SUBSEQUENT YEARS.

1775–1785.

Again, dear Reader the clairon of war
has sounded ; again the rocky heights of
Cape Diamond echo to the shrill call
of military horn and bugle. Not even
the ice-bound river and the snow-buried
plain, have secured the Country from an
invasion, in the name of liberty ! But is
the peaceful cloister again to be disturbed,
its inmates scattered, its walls ruined ?
We have just perused the narrative,
Mother St. Etienne has left of this American invasion of 1775, the fourth siege
the Convent has witnessed. [1]

Our readers would find nothing new
to them in the details she furnishes of

[1] The sieges of 1690, 1759, 1760 and 1775.

that daring attack upon Quebec, except what regards the Convent ; and to this we shall mainly confine ourselves. It would be needless to follow the vicissitudes of that campaign, undertaken with the mistaken idea that Canada would willingly join the American Colonies in their attempt to throw off the British yoke. History has traced the march of the invading army, which, under Montgomery, bore off the British colors from every fort and town in its path.—St. John's, Chambly, Sorel, Montreal, Three-Rivers,—till joining that other hardy band that issued from the woods on the banks of the river Chaudière, they hasten on, cheering loudly as they pause before the gates of Quebec, expecting to see them thrown open to its deliverers ! The issue of that midnight strife of December, 1775, was written in bloody characters, upon the banks of freshly fallen snow, with the fate of the gallant but unfortunate Montgomery. The memory of all this has been lately revived by a commemorative centennial. We need not dwell upon

the winter's blockade ; the arrival in
March of an English fleet, bringing timely
succor to the weary garrison ; the final
evacuation of Canada by the American
forces :—we are certain to gratify our
readers more, by opening to their view
the interior of the cloister during that six
months' Siege.

We shall not find a flock of young and
timid doves, to be frightened by the first
discharge of artillery. No! many of these
thirty-four professed nuns had been
through scenes that had given them
courage and experience; they remembered the two Sieges of 1759 and 1760,
and trusted themselves all the more se-
renely to the protecting care of Divine
Providence. Beyond the walls along the
suburb of St. Roch, and in the Intendant's
palace, in full view of the Convent, there
were some hundreds of armed men, raising batteries and pointing cannon upon
the town : when these preparations are
completed the murderous projectiles are
scattered like hail-stones all around the
premises, but they do not appear unused

to the smoke and din of war! One of the
nuns, as she was passing through an
apartment, had a piece of her apron carried away by a cannon-ball;—it is not
related whether she even kept the frag-
ment as a souvenir! [1]

Let us hear Reverend Mother St. Louis
de Gonzague, giving a summary account
of the winter to the Ursulines of Paris:—

"We would be most ungrateful, she
says, if we did not bless a thousand times
the Author of all good, who supports and
consoles his servants in the midst of the
different trials of this life. Your fervent
prayers, my dear Mothers, obtained for
us new courage, which transformed us
all into heroines. You are aware we
have passed through a six months' Siege.
I leave you to imagine the feelings of
poor nuns in such circumstances, with
the fire of the combat constantly before
their eyes, and threatened at every moment by the bombs and cannon balls.
The first ball that reached us, struck the
Infirmary; another entered the novitiate,

[1] See note C in Appendix.

breaking the windows, and a novice's bed. We hastened to take out the window sashes, and this being perceived by the enemy, they lowered their guns. Evidently, they did not intend to harm us.

"A little later, a ball passed through the church windows, and struck a neighboring house. The Almighty protected us, taking pity on poor nuns, who have no other part in war but to suffer its inevitable penalties. However courageous we may have felt, it must be owned that the situation was not an agreeable one. To live amid constant alarms, announced by the tocsin—the bells ringing only on these occasions—to be stunned, night and day, by the rolling of drums and the booming of cannon, to have no place of safety in case of danger, our only vault (which served as a chapel) being fractured and insecure ;—all this was not pleasant.

"On the 15th December we had our elections, in military style, to the sound of guns and cannon !

"Our observances were followed regu-

larly, in chapel, in spite of the rigors of
the season. All these inconveniences
have not sufficed to incommode the health
of any one of us seriously, which certainly seems wonderful. It is true we had
the advantage of being all together, at
home, without anxiety for our subsistence,
our prudent *Depositaire* having laid in a
good store of provisions; which was no
small relief and aid in supporting the miseries entailed by war." Oh! we may well
say " There's no place like home " since
the casualties of war itself can be affront-
ed with intrepidity by the aid of mutual
sympathy and charity !

After an interval of ten years (1785) if
we enquire, How fares the Convent? we
find the nuns yet struggling with poverty, sharing the difficulties that, on all
sides, weighed heavily on the Country.
Governor Haldimand was not the man
to bring order and good-feeling, out of
confusion and dissatisfaction. To the
misery caused by the want of public confidence, scarcity of money, and high rates
for merchandise of every kind, were

added other calamities; bad seasons, poor crops, shipwrecks, and accidents. Even the moral atmosphere was dark and lowering. See the following extract from a letter written in 1785 to the Ursulines of Paris.

" We have reason to weep in the sight of Heaven over our poor Country. There is liberty, it is true, to profess our holy Religion. but there is little care for living piously or fulfilling the duties of a Christian. The young girls who are confided to us for their education. have not been brought up as they were formerly Then, after their first Communion, they are taken from us to be introduced into society and to frequent the theatre You may easily suppose the sad results of these dangerous amusements. If I enter into these details —to which much more might be added — it is to-engage you to offer your fervent prayers for us, and for our poor people." In another letter, she writes : " Luxury and vanity are the order of the day ; yet there are many good, pious souls, who persevere faithful to duty."

A want which from year to year was deplored by the Ursulines as well as by every other Institution for education, was the dearth of French books for the pupils. All direct communications with France had ceased; and printing was yet on a small scale in Canada. One French librarian in Paris, was known, who had a correspondent in London; through him, from time to time, the educational establishments here, could renew their class-books; but the limited importation was subject to many inconveniences.

The decline of piety, the difficulties of various kinds already enumerated, and others too long to be detailed here, had the effect of diminishing the number of boarders towards the close of the century. The course of studies became more and more elementary. and for a great many only extended to the period of their first Communion.

On the other hand, more and more alarming were the reports that came from

Europe, of the growth of infidelity, irre-
ligion, and crime, especially in France,
that France which, to our nuns, was still
the beloved mother-country. Already
the suppression of the Jesuits (1773), and
that of other religious Orders in subsequent years, gave but too evident signs
of the profound depravity of those men
who had placed themselves at the head
of the revolutionary movement.

Alas! for that ill-fated Country; there
were days in store for her people, darker
than those which in 1785 [1] terrified the
comparatively innocent population of Canada, and of which we are forcibly reminded, as we revert to that period of
moral darkness, "the Reign of Terror."

---

[1] See note D in Appendix.

CHAPTER XIII.

REV. MOTHER ESTHER WHEELWRIGHT, AND
OTHER SUPERIORS:

AMICABLE RELATIONS WITH THE ENGLISH
GOVERNORS.

1760—1799.

A Superioress bearing an English name,
appearing for the first time in the Community just as English rule is being inaugurated in Canada, seems a strange coin-
cidence ; but you are aware, dear Reader, that Mother Wheelwright of the Infant Jesus was so thoroughly naturalized
a French lady, that she had no longer
the use of her native tongue.

This child of Providence, whom you
have recognized as the *Indian Captive*,
had never been forgotten in the home of
her infancy. If the difficulty of communication between the city of Boston and
Quebec, at that time, prevented the be-

reaved parents from satisfying their affection by coming to see their daughter,
they lost no opportunity of reminding
her by letters and by presents of their
tender remembrance. Among these souvenirs, none surely was so precious as the
miniature portrait of her beloved mother
—which is still preserved in the Convent.

Nearly fifty years had separated Mother
Wheelwright of the Infant Jesus from
her family, when a nephew of hers, having performed the long journey expressly
to see his Aunt, was admitted to visit her
within the cloister. On taking leave of
his newly-found relative, Mr. Wheelwright, regardless of her objections, on
the score of her vow of poverty, placed in
her hands a silver cover and goblet, in
the name of her family.

A few months after our amiable Mother's re-election in 1764, occurred the
Golden Jubilee of her religious profession,
our Church being at that time still open
to the public for the parish Offices. According to the Annalist, nothing was

wanting to enhance the solemnity of the fête ;— the organ, played by the Chaplain, Reverend M. Resche ; good and devout singing, by the best voices in the Community ; an eloquent sermon on the happiness of the religious life : the morning ceremony concluded with the *Te Deum*, and that of the afternoon with the Benediction of the Blessed Sacrament.

These details show that the usual pious rejoicings on such occasions, were not interrupted by the presence in the Country of a hostile creed ; the "Hind and Panther" were not growling at each other— openly at least

Let the old Manuscript we love to refer to, tell what opinion the companions of Mother Esther of the Infant Jesus, had formed of her virtues as a religious. Oh! they are eloquent on praising that "soul predestined from all eternity, the beloved of God and man, whose admirable examples during her long career of sixty-eight years, spent in the service of her Divine Master in this community, have a more touching language than all that could be written.

" It is true she had been endowed with the happiest of dispositions and an excellent constitution ; but to what a holy use did she not apply these precious gifts, walking firmly in the path of perfection ; strictly observing the minutest points of the rule, placing in this, as she said herself, her joy and consolation. Every thing that tended to the glory of God inflamed her zeal. What pains did she not take in instructing young girls, during the many years she was employed in that department ! If her extreme gentleness, her grace, her exquisite politeness, rendered it difficult for her to take upon herself that tone of authority which is sometimes necessary, she always succeeded in gaining the esteem, respect and affection of the pupils. Her qualifications admirably fitted her for the offices to which she was called in the interior of the Monastery, as Superior, Assistant,

Zelatrix, and Mistress of novices. Laborious at all times, it was particularly during the years of penury and distress for the Convent, that this beloved Mother exerted her skill in embroidery and fancy-work, in order to contribute to the support of the Community. When her sight had become too feeble to permit her to execute these more delicate labors of the needle, she solicited and obtained leave, to do the mending of the house, displaying in this such neatness, economy, and amiability that every one admired her; yet this is not snrprising when we know what purity of intention and interior spirit animated all her actions."

If St. Bernard hesitates not to ascribe the merit of martyrdom to the religious life. persevered in to the end with fervor, what must not be the recompense of this privileged soul, who sacrificing home and country, devoted herself unreservedly to the service of her Divine Master, only laying down the Cross with her life, at the age of eighty-four years "It was on the 20th of October 1780, amid her usual aspirations towards Heaven, that our beloved Mother Wheelwright of the Infant Jesus ceased to live in this world, to live for ever with the Blessed in heaven, leaving us the legacy of her virtues to imitate, and a, memory that will be ever fresh in our grateful hearts. Her ancestors were noble, as the arms of her family bear witness, but she needed not the illustration of birth or title, to win from all who knew her a willing tribute of love and admiration."

With the name of Mother Esther of the Infant Jesus, we naturally associate that of Mother Davanne of St. Louis de Gonzague, these two remarkable Superiors having shared the office during eighteen years (1760.1778), continuing the amicable relations with the new Government, commenced so auspiciously under Mother Rev. Migeon of the Nativity.

We here find ourselves in presence of

a Parisian lady, and at the same time we are reminded of a domestic drama, stranger than fiction, for which we must refer our readers to a future page ; the present must be confined to what regards Mother St. Louis de Gonzague as Superioress, recalling some furthur instances of the kind feeling with which the Ursulines were regarded by Governor Carleton,—later, Lord Dorchester—and by all his honorable family, as well as by the other Officers of his British Majesty in Quebec.

It is well known that Sir Guy Carleton was a sincere and constant friend of the Canadians, or as our Annalist says, that " he was justly beloved by all classes of people. His mild and paternal administration, his prudence and benevolence, his personal merits and kindness, rendered him dear to all ranks. Long may it please the King to continue him in office ! " she adds with emphasis.

The relations of Lady Carleton with the inmates of the cloister, were most intimate and cordial.

It was through her influence, and at the request of Governor Carleton, that the nuns consented to admit as parlor-boarder,[1] a relative of the family, Mrs. Johnston, while her husband was absent in London. The same favor, which at the present day, is refused to more than one applicant, was again granted, later, (1778) to the widow of Major Carleton, Lady Anne. This lady, whose fine qualities and rare amiability endeared her much to the nuns, became so attached to them and to her secluded way of living under the Convent roof, that she would willingly have arranged to make her situation a permanent one. She finally decided to rejoin her family in London, leaving with as much regret as the nuns themselves felt to part with her.

Lady Carleton was, at all times, most

---

[1] Mrs. Johnston, as well as Lady Carleton, occupied the apartment that has since become the Chaplain's room. It was then, as now, beyond the limits of the strict cloister.

gracious and obliging, bringing her little family to see the nuns, visiting them first on her arrival, and last on leaving the country each time that she had to cross the Ocean. On one of these parting occasions, accompanied by her suite, and by her "three little sons, also her little daughter whom we had not yet seen," she presented the Mother Superior with two silver candlesticks for the Church. The nuns rightly said, that a Catholic could not have been more thoughtful and delicate in the choice of a parting souvenir.

Praising the governor's wise administration, and wishing that his successor may follow in his footsteps, our Annalist adds : " He has governed the country with admirable prudence, and given proof of greatness of soul in many critical moments ; he has labored indefatigably to promote the welfare and best interests of the people, treating the Bishop and Clergy with deference and esteem, and suffering no one to be molested on account of his religion."

Then with what hearty expressions the same pen records in 1786, the "return of my Lord Dorchester our ancient Governor to the great joy of the Clergy, as well as the people. He was hailed by a salute of artillery and received by the troops under arms. My Lady, after suffering much from the sea-voyage has arrived in good health with all her family."

On her first visit to her cloistered friends, Lady Dorchester signified her desire that her daughter should take lessons in French and in embroidery from the nuns. Accordingly, with the authorization of Bishop Briand, the young Countess was admitted daily, for the space of two or three hours, her mother accompanying her in order to enjoy the amiable company of the French teacher, Mother Davanne of St. Louis de Gonzague, and to perfect herself in the French language.

At all times, a visit to the Ursulines seems to have been a part of the programme of the Governor's reception in Quebec.

Returning now to our theme, after this long digression, we meet a new Superior in the person of Mother Antoinette Poulin of St. Francis. Like Mother La Grange of St. Louis, it was chiefly as *Dépositaire*, during long years of penury and difficulties of every kind, that Mother St. Francis has acquired a right to the perpetual gratitude of her Community. Much of her voluminous correspondence with the Ursulines of France having been preserved, we are enabled to enter into an intimate acquaintance with the amiable Mother, who from 1760 to 1787 was the visible Providence of the Monastery. The clearness and precision of her style, the elevation of her sentiments, the sensibility of her heart, in turn, excite our admiration, revealing her character precisely as her biographer has traced it. We readily understand that "this dear Mother was moved with a tender compassion for the afflicted, being charitable and kind to all. During the twenty-one years that she was charged with our temporal affairs, in times of the greatest difficulty, her economy and foresight were admirable; but her goodness of heart was still greater, and of this we were so well persuaded that it served to moderate the sufferings of that memorable period. She was one of the eight courageous Sisters who remained during the Siege to watch over the Monastery. She loved the pupils tenderly, and manifested her affection on every occasion, not only when employed with them in teaching, but in every office that had the least relation with that duty, the dearest and most important for an Ursuline." At the age of sixty-five, having filled the measure of her days and of her merits, Mother St. Francis, passed to a better life (1790).

Mother Brassard of St. Clare held the office of Superior from 1787 to 1793. In her, we recognize a daughter of one of those ancient and honorable families, fortunately not rare in Canada, from whose pious ranks the Divine Master loves to recruit new laborers for his vineyard. How glorious is such a distinction! What a treasure of heavenly blessings upon the

rest of the family, is the sure recompense
of parents who generously give to God the
son who was their pride and stay, or the
daughter who, above all, was their solace
and their joy. In the present instance,
while two sisters consecrate their lives to
God as Ursulines, their brother [1] becomes
a priest, and endows his country with a
new Institution for learning and piety.

Mother St. Clare is described by her
contemporaries as "one of those rare persons in whom the solid virtues were
united to distinguished talents ; who governed others without detriment to her
own perfection, possessing the secret of
winning the love and respect of her in-
feriors, maintaining with an equal hand,
charity, union and the observance of the
rule. All the virtues shone in her daily
life, yet, above them all, her humility
was conspicuous."

It was while Mother Brassard of St.

[1] Rev. L. Brassard, founded the college of Nicolet in
1804. Marie-Anne Brassard of St. Madeleine entered
the Convent in 1755, being the last to make profession before the Conquest. She lived to 1815, having
witnessed the three Sieges of Quebec.

Clare was Superior, that the Monastery celebrated on the 1st of August, 1789, its 150th Anniversary. The Centennial had found the church in all the glow of its fresh finishing; but the last half-century had been a rough one, and some reparations were required. These had been attended to from the month of May, in order to perform with " as much splendor as circumstances would allow " the stately ceremonies by which Religion comes to our aid, when we would publicly testify our gratitude to the Most High. " We had High Mass, say the Annals, Benediction of the Blessed Sacrament, and a solemn *Te Deum*, to thank God for all the blessings showered down upon this House since its foundation. Mgr. de Capse, the newly consecrated Bishop, kindly offered to officiate. Several Clergymen, uniting in our intentions, celebrated Mass in our Chapel. We sang hymns and canticles of joy and gratitude, thanking God with all our hearts for preserving our Community, especially since we are under the dominion of Great Britain "

CHAPTER XIV.

SAD ECHOES OF THE FRENCH REVOLUTION.

1793–1802.

The ties that bound our Ursulines to France, were not only those of consanguinity and affection, like all the other French inhabitants of Canada. There was another link, peculiar to their profession : it was the sweet fraternal bond of charity, by which the members of our dear Lord's chosen friends, cherish each other, in very truth, as brethren and sisters.

In Paris, that centre where the Revolution had established its stronghold, were two flourishing Convents of the Order of St. Ursula. One of these was not only the *Alma Mater* of all the Convents of the "*Congregation of Paris*" in France, but had become, by adoption, the Mother-

House of the Ursulines of Quebec. Our readers remember that after the Monastery of Tours had furnished the two pillars of the edifice, in the persons of Mother Marie de l'Incarnation and Mother St. Joseph, the greater number of the other devoted nuns from France, have been designated by us as Parisians. In 1682, the union was consummated by the Ursulines of Quebec adopting the Constitution of the Ursulines of Paris. During all this period of a century and a half, the correspondence had ever been most cordial,—fraternal, in every sense of the word.

Great, then, was the anxiety of our Ursulines of Quebec for the fate of their beloved Sisters in France generally; but for those of Paris, especially, on account of their greater danger, and the more intimate relations that existed between them. " Fatal and terrible Revolution, writes the Annalist in 1794, which has accumulated woes without number for the Church and for the human race; which in its efforts to destroy Religion has put an end to the Monarchy; led to the scaffold the King and the most illustrious members of the Royal family; raised aloft the standard of Atheism; overturned churches and altars; pillaged and profaned the sacred vessels; massacred the priests; depopulated the cloisters: in a word, caused so many evils and horrors that my pen would refuse to retrace them."

Meanwhile the dismal years of that last decade of the eighteenth century roll on, bearing distress and bloodshed from the frontiers of France through the finest countries of Europe. Rome is taken; the Holy Father, at the age of eighty-one, is a prisoner, an exile; till, finally, offering his life for his flock, the illustrious Pontiff, the Father of the Faithful, closes his eyes in death, a last victim to impiety, injustice, and ambition.

Through all these years which, for good Catholics, for all, indeed, who had not lost the sense of ordinary humanity, were truly years of bitterness, while they were years of suffering for virtue and innocence, what had been the fate of the

Ursulines of Paris ? When all Religious Orders had been proscribed by these red-revolutionaries, when the monastic habit and profession had been made a crime against the State, when hundreds of priests, monks, and nuns, had expiated on the scaffold the offence of being guilt-less, — had the Ursulines escaped with impunity ?

The last letter our nuns had received from their dear Sisters, was dated the 18th February, 1791.—It was almost entirely devoted to business-matters, rents in arrears, &c., for the Ursulines of Quebec had property in France, now ready to be engulfed, with all other Church property, by the torrent of the Revolution. " We live in sad times, we are in need of faith and confidence. I say nothing of our fears......... the public papers will tell you enough—Pray for us, we are much in need of your prayers."…. Such had been the laconic message, in which anxiety and sad forebodings are but too evident. No further tidings tra-versed the Ocean during eleven long years.

At last,—it was in 1802—an English merchant had brought out from London a parcel, addressed to the Ursulines of Quebec ; and he called at the Convent to say that it had been found accidentally, having been forgotten by the shop-keeper to whom it had been confided by some French exiles, nine years previous. The paper was yellow and dust-stained ; the handwriting, heavy and trembling. " The date was January, 13th, 1793, " and was signed—" De Lange de St. Augustin, Ex-Superior of the Ursulines of the Suburb St. Jacques, Paris." The second bore the signature :—" P. de B. (Picard de Beaucacour) dite de Ste. Cécile."

Let us quote the touching details of their irreparable misfortunes :—

" You have doubtless heard, with grief, dear Reverend Mothers, of the devastation and destruction of all Religious Houses. Our Monastery, which was one of the best established and best regulated in France, has not escaped the common fate. Your compassionate hearts would have bled to see the cloister-wall broken down, and ourselves forcibly driven from our peaceful asylum, to seek refuge wherever we could find some charitable soul to receive us. To our great regret, we are all scattered. Pity us, dear Mothers, and beg our Divine Lord to grant us the grace to make a holy use of the heavy trial he has sent us.

" All the Clergy with whom we were acquainted, have disappeared, and it is impossible to discover who escaped the massacre of the 24th September. Our venerable Confessor and our two Chaplains were certainly among the victims.— I cannot enter into further details. Ask our dear Lord to give me perfect resignation."...... The aged Mother Superior concludes with these words :—" I recommend myself to your good prayers as one already dead, for although my health is pretty good, which seems a miracle considering my seventy-four years, and my cruel situation, I may not be among the living when this reaches you. The holy will of God be done. If I were younger, I think I would accept your invitation."

... ... were ... in great part
... ... of our Monastery. Their
own resources would not make these
... ... in their
power to prevent their Canadian Sisters'
interests from suffering. The ...
... Mother St. Suzanne, who had been
... Louisiana in Paris for twenty years,
was now seventy-one years of age, and
... ... Lodged in
... ... beyond
... ... was attended by the
... ... who had removed
... ... It is the charitable in-
... ...

... Mother St. Suzanne is declining
... ... there is no hope of her recovery. She is very suffering, but gentle,
patient, and resigned to the will of our
blessed Master. Her state is a daily subject
of meditation for me. I beg you to offer
your most fervent prayers for her, beloved
Mothers. She often thinks of you, and
speaks of her dear Quebec Sisters, in a
manner that shows how much she loves
. She tells me, if she were in a state

to be able to profit of your obliging invitation, she would do so with much gratitude. I share her sentiments : we all share them. What a contrast between our present position, and the time when we could make others happy ! But, my good Mothers, we must adore with submission the orders of Divine Providence, convinced that every thing that happens in this world is destined to serve for our salvation......"

Let us hasten to the conclusion of the sad drama. The dear sufferer, so meek beneath the stroke that banished her from her peaceful cloister in her old age, had gone to a better life a few days after the date of the letter we have just quoted. Her charitable companion rejoined the venerable Superior, who finally succeeded in gathering quietly around her, the scattered members of her spiritual family. It was in their midst that, four years later, her dear soul, doubly purified by affliction and patience, took its flight towards heaven. Still the exiled Ursulines continued to sigh for their cloister, and to watch for an opportunity to return to the field of their former labors; employing themselves, meanwhile, with joy, in teaching the poor children they could assemble. But it was not in Paris, that centre of the revolutionary madness which had overturned both throne and altar, that, so soon, could be found a place for the daughters of St. Angela—the avowed apostles of virtue and Religion. One by one the links of that bright chain were broken by death, till in 1830, there were only two remaining: and, in 1835, a voyager from Quebec[1] was introduced to the last survivor of the Ursulines of Paris......This venerable lady of eighty-five, still bright in her intellect and clear in her faculties, had been one of the last to make profession in that noble Institution before the fierce tornado of the Revolution had passed, burying so much happiness, so many hopes, under the ruins of so many Sanctuaries!

[1] Rev. Th. Maguire, V. G. of the Diocese of Quebec, and Chaplain of the Ursulines.

[2] In 1806, an Imperial Decree authorized the Ursulines to assemble in Communities, but failed to

CHAPTER XV.

CONTRASTED SCENES, IN THE LIFE OF MOTHER DAVANNE OF ST. LOUIS DE GONZAGUE.

1800.

On the evening of the third of February, 1800, one who had entered the silent Chapel of the Ursuline Convent, at a quarter to six P. M., would have found it, as is usual at that hour, vacant and in obscurity, save the one starry light, gleaming before the Tabernacle, announcing the MASTER'S PRESENCE there. But, no!—another glance shows the kneeling form of an aged Nun, and by her side a diminutive lantern, whose tiny flame might barely serve to guide her footseps in the dark of early mornings, or when the

restore to them their Convents and property of which the Revolution had despoiled them. In 1810 the Ursulines of Paris were living at Puteaux, near Neuilly. In 1828, the few survivors were lodged in Vaugirard street, St. Germain suburb. Finally, in 1835, only one,—Mother St. Angela—remained,—as is stated above.

evening rings the call to prayer. At this
unwonted hour for a visit to the Chapel,
Mother Davanne of St. Louis de Gonzague
only remains a few moments in silent ad-
oration, and rises to retire. As she mounts
the stairs that lead to the Community-Hall,
she is met by a smiling band, and escorted as in triumph.

The double-door, opening wide, discov-
ers all the Sisterhood assembled, waiting
to greet the venerable Mother, who, for
eight days past, has been in retreat, preparing to renew in the fervor of her first
profession those vows she pronounced sixty years ago. How joyous, is each beaming countenance in this real family-circle,
where presides, in sweet maternal dignity,
Reverend Mother Marchand of St. Ursula;
and where are so many others, whose
names are still so familiar to us all :—
Mothers Panet of St. Bernard and St.
James, Dubé of St. Ignatius, Berthelot
of St. Joseph, La Ferrière of Ste. Marie.
Here also, for this occasion, are the ami-
te-veiled novices, Sisters Mc-
of St. Henry and Dougherty of

St. Augustin. With what fervor Mother
Giroux des Anges has entoned that soul-
thrilling chant : " ECCE QUAM BONUM,"
in which she is joined by the choir, in
accents that make us realize indeed, how
*good and pleasant a thing it is to dwell to-
gether in unity !*

This is but the prelude of the morrow's
celebration, when the more sacred and
solemn part being over, this most amiable
and beloved Mother will again be the
object of all the demonstrations of joy and
affection, which it has been possible for
grateful hearts to invent. *

The decorations of the Hall are already
complete. The figure **60**, traced in flowers and lighted tapers, crowns the honored
NAME, equally glowing and conspicuous;
the carpeted steps of the throne over
which a delicate canopy is suspended ;
the gay banners inscribed with mottoes ;
the fragrant evergreens hung with lamps,
and blossoming, in spite of nature and
the rude season ; the moss-grown seats
and gay parterre, where to-morrow

nymphs and maidens will vocalize in joyous groups :—every thing is express-ive of the kind feeling that prompts these innocent festivities. Nor song, nor poem, nor enthusiastic address, nor ingenious device, will be wanting.

Reverend Mother Superior herself has arranged the programme; the Bishop elect will preside; a numerous Clergy after celebrating the Mysteries of Religion to call down new graces on this beloved *senior* of the Community will be there :—but, Reader, instead of awaiting the varied entertainment, let us turn to scenes far different from these, yet scenes in which the Convent heroine of this 4th of Febru-ary, 1800, had a deep, and sometimes a most painful part.

A domestic drama—we have said on another page—is connected with the dear name of Mother Davanne of St. Louis de Gonzague. Its commencement leads us away to Paris; that gay, fascinating, fickle, and sometimes terrible Capital, of which Frenchmen are nevertheless so proud.

There, in 1719, Marie Marguerite Davanne was born, of respectable and
wealthy parents, and there she passed
the first years of her childhood.

Some commercial transaction, however,
in which Mr. Davanne was engaged, entailed the ruin of his fortune ; and induced
him, with the little he had saved from
the wreck of his hopes, to seek the shores
of Canada. Bringing his family with him,
he fixed his residence at the Lower Town,
Quebec. The late Parisian bankrupt was
active and enterprising, his business pros-
pered, and in a short time he had repaired
his losses sufficiently to enable him to live
as comfortably as before. Unfortunately,
the passion of getting rich, induced him
to risk again, in some speculation, all he
had acquired.—The enterprise failing,
again he lost all. This time, he resolved
to try his fortune, unattended by his family, and embarked for the East Indies.
Mrs. Davanne had, apparently, a moderate
pension of her own; at all events, she
was powerless to dissuade her husband

from that long sea-voyage, destined to be so fatal to the happiness of both. Bidding adieu to his wife and children, for a year, the insolvent merchant lightly stepped on board; the good ship weighed anchor, and spreading her sails, soon lost sight of the clustering houses of Lower Town, that spot which contained all that the voyager held most dear.

We know not to which party that year seemed longest; but no news from either side once broke its tediousness.

Another and another year passed by, and yet no news of ship or traveller reached Quebec. Anxious and desponding, the unhappy woman resolved to return to France; there, at least, she might obtain some tidings of the tragical end of her husband, whom already she firmly believed to be lost. Marie-Marguerite, then about eighteen years of age, had been to the Convent school the greater part of the time since the arrival of the family in Quebec; she had meditated her consecration to God : and now, in the alternative of leaving the country, she threw herself at her mother's feet, begging leave to rejoin her beloved teachers, and to make the Monastery her future home.

Mrs. Davanne could not refuse her consent, and adding this new sacrifice to the rest, came with her daughter to make the demand and arrange for her entrance. Unable to pay the accustomed dowry in full, Mrs. Davanne offered what she could spare ; and leaving her own portrait as the dearest souvenir to her beloved child, she bade her the last farewell, promising to write on her arrival in Paris, but uncertain whether or not she would ever return to Canada. In Paris, neither the family nor friends of Mr. Davanne had heard of him. His fate was a mystery ; but the length of time he had been absent was sufficient to confirm Mrs. Davanne's fears of the worst ;—doubtless he had perished. Friends, with officious kindness, surround the supposed widow, who was still young, and rich in that most dangerous of gifts, personal attractions. They finally persuaded her that it would not only be right to accept, but, that it would be folly for her to refuse, the offers of the rich Parisian who awaited her hand. The unfortunate lady pronounced the fatal word of consent ; and the marriage was celebrated. Scarcely had the echo of the brilliant wedding passed by, than a vague and suspicious rumor began to circulate. In a brief space it changed to certainty :—Mr. Davanne was still living !

He had been shipwrecked in his voyage from Quebec, but not lost, nor discouraged. With that indomitable energy which characterized him, he had pursued his plans and found means to retrieve his ruined fortune. He had written many times to his family, but, by some fatality, no letter had reached its distination.

Informed of his wife's return to Paris, just as he was on the point of leaving India, he determined to be himself the messenger of a brighter future—when on a sudden he heard the fatal news of the marriage she had just contracted.

Taking counsel only of his disappointment, and the fury inspired by the supposed outrage, he hastens to lay the case, in the blackest colors, before the tribunals of justice; the hapless victim of her own imprudence, more guilty before the law than before her own conscience, is condemned to perpetual seclusion......

While we hesitate to decide which of the two unfortunates is most to be pitied, let us return to their well-beloved daughter, who, in the peaceful cloister where she is daily making new progress in perfection, is far from presaging the terrible storm that has burst over heads so dear, or the pitiless stroke that is awaiting her own innocent heart.

One afternoon, a parcel of letters from France is opened at the Mother Superior's room. Among the different addresses, is the name of Mlle. Marie Marguerite Davanne. Mother Migeon of the Nativity sends for the dear Novice, whose anxiety to hear from her mother, all knew and shared. They commenced reading the letter together, but as the terrible truth,

at first not fully realized, begins to be understood, a convulsive trembling seizes
the frame of that unfortunate child of
most unhappy parents ; the troubled
heart refusing the bitter draught, the
limbs relax and the semblance of death
ensues.   Oh! well might the first tidings
of such an excess of misery overcome the
fortitude of one so unprepared for grief!
When recovered from her faint, she feels
the solace of the sympathy, sincere and
enlightened, which surrounds her; yet
the following day told what had been the
interior struggle in the acceptance of
that cup, bitterer than death itself.   The
young novice who on retiring to her cell
that night had lifted her veil from a head
as dark as the raven's wing, rose next
morning with the silvery crown old age
is wont to bestow :—such was the effect
of that one night of sorrow !

We need not ask what had been her
reflections....... In after years, she was
often heard to say : "It was at the age of
twenty-one, that I began to truly appreciate the happiness of the Religious state."

Yes ! henceforth she knew the treach-
erous fragility of the dearest earthly ties ;
and spurning every thing that savored
of the world, she aspired to nothing less
than the most intimate friendship with
that ONE HEART that does not change,
but ever overflows with tenderness for
each one of us his creatures.

The long career of Mother Davanne de
St. Louis de Gonzague extended to the
eighty-second year of her age, and was
full of good works and of merit in the
sight of Heaven. She preserved to the
end, the perfect use of her faculties, the
freshness of her youthful piety and
fervor, the cheerfulness and amiability
which had made her life like a perpetual
sunshine in the midst of her Sisters.

If the portrait of Madame Davanne [1]

[1] The portrait of Madame Davanne—an oil-painting of merit—represents her in her youth, habited
in a Greek costume : the painter by giving her a
palm, has transformed the lovely nymph into a St.
Catherine. It was a device not uncommon in the
18th century, as a means of enabling a family-por-
trait to be preserved.

has been preserved in the Monastery to
the present day, it is not surprising that
the hand of tradition has seized upon the
most salient traits of the daughter's picture to present them to posterity.

According to this tradition, Mother
St. Louis de Gonzague was the *beau ideal*
of all that is most charming in a woman :
a dignified and agreeable stature, an easy
carriage, with every grace of manners
and speech; an intellectual face, in which
if the chisel found a faultless model,
the artist might despair to render the
expression—combining meekness, benevolence, a tender compassion for every
human woe and an ardent love of God.

Besides this portrait of the exterior,
another more prized has been preserved,
telling of faithfulness to grace, zeal for
the glory of God and the good of souls ;—
of the manifold duties of the religious life
accomplished with a pure intention in
the sight of Heaven, regardless of personal satisfaction or comfort, during that
long and useful career. The gratitude

of the Community is particularly due to
Mother St. Louis de Gonzague for the
fifteen years of her administration as Superior; for the courage she displayed at
the epoch of the Siege of 1759, when with
a little band she remained to guard the
Convent from utter devastation ; for her
arduous labors in the other offices, in all
of which her prudence and charity, with a
boundless love for her Community, were
most conspicuous.

One day the whole household were
assembled around the aged and beloved
Mother, as we have seen, to congratulate
her on the second recurrence of her
golden Jubilee. Among the Poems on
that occasion there was one in the form of
an Enigma, that describes, in another
light, Mother St. Louis de Gonzague :
with this little Poem we shall take our
leave of her name.   It is entitled—

THE PIOUS SECRET.

" On earth to live, all creatures try ;—
For me, I only seek to die.
Trials and sufferings I endure,
And thus from evil keep me pure :

The greatest enemy I know,
Is self,—that is my real foe.
Death waits for mortals at life's end ;
For me, I die each day I spend.
Although my soul endures the while,
Imprisoned in the body vile,
She loves to lift her pinions high,
And sail unfettered to the sky.
To God, my all I gladly give !
I live—no, 'tis not I that live
It is—but I too much have told,
The secret you may well unfold !
Guess what it is.　Well, have you said ?
Do tell us,—if all doubts have fled.
Have you divined ?　' O yes, 'tis clear,
It is a soul to Heaven most dear,—
Some Saint, perhaps.' You're on the road ;
One trial more, you'll have it good ;
Never enigma was so plain.
Come, Reverend Mother, try again !
Truly, my patience can no longer wait.
It is YOURSELF !—the portrait is no feint."

GLAPION, S. J.

CHAPTER XVI.

SUPERIORS OF THE 19TH CENTURY:

REV. MOTHERS MARCHAND OF ST. URSULA AND TASCHEREAU OF ST. FRANCOIS-XAVIER.

1793-1818.

We are approaching modern times, kind Reader. The chain of tradition, strong and bright, lies as it were within our grasp, and we are about to confide it with affectionate care to the keeping of those who will come after us. This 19th century, up to the date of 1871, presents us a group of seven Superiors; the only surviving one—a contemporary of all the others — is our beloved and venerated Mother St. Gabriel, now eighty years of age.

It is a goodly and cheering picture as we bring before us the leading traits that distinguished these worthy Mothers—the three last, Mothers St. Henry, St. Andrew and St. Gabriel being of our own day :

the countenance, equally humble, mild
and serene; the smile that told of a heart
overflowing with charity; the care and
foresight truly maternal, that forgot no
one, and overlooked no want; the encouraging spur of a living Rule, which
their lives ever offered : while they were
for us the oracle of God, declaring to us
from day to day His holy will in our
regard.

The most distant figure of the group is
Rev. Mother Taschereau of St. Francis-
Xavier, first called to the superiority in.
1793, and re-elected at various periods, till
she had governed fifteen years.

Rev. Mother Marchand of St. Ursula,
charged in 1799, by the unanimous voice
of her Sisters to succeed Mother St.
Xavier, opens the century under the happiest auspices. The name of both these
worthy Mothers, still fresh among us and
held in veneration, are synonymous with
all that is most honorable in family de-
scent. in amiable qualities and natural
    s well as with all that is most

edifying and exemplary in the life of a holy Religious.

Mother St. Ursula, known in the world as Miss Marie-Marguerite Marchand, was a native of Verchères, and a descendant of the family de Boucherville, by her mother Marguerite Boucher de Niverville. While yet a novice, under the excellent training of Mother Davanne of St. Louis de Gonzague, she gave evidence of that maturity of judgment, and those inestimable qualities of the mind and heart which rendered her so precious to the Community, whether in the noble function of teacher, or in the other offices to which she was occasionally appointed.

The Annals, deploring her premature loss in 1815, depict her as one of the pillars of the monastery.

" In this incomparable Mother, says the writer, we had a Superior, who in her government gave universal satisfaction. Noble and generous in mind, prepossessing in manners, as capable for business as she was amiable and cheerful

in conversation ;—her agreeable and expressive countenance was the exact index
of her soul. Her piety was solid and
enlightened, her gentleness unfailing, her
courage magnanimous.

" Mother St. Ursula had just been re-
elected as Superior for the fourth time,
when she was attacked by that cruel malady, inflammatory rheumatism. During
nine weeks, she had hardly a moment's
respite from multiplied and intense sufferings. Thus she became a living copy
of her patroness, St. Ursula, meriting
by her invincible patience to be associated to the Martyr's crown. "

Neither the best medical attendance,
nor the sympathy of friends of every rank
who united their prayers to those of the
afflicted Community, was sufficient to
arrest or delay the progress of the cruel
malady. Among the many kind letters
addressed to the dear sufferer, there was
one which she requested to hear again
and again : it was from the celebrated
Abbé de Calonne, who resided, at the time,

at Three Rivers. The letter has been carefully preserved, and is so replete with Christian consolation and encouragement that we have thought fit to transcribe a few lines.

After testifying the liveliest interest in the recovery of the venerated patient, the Abbé exclaims : — " Ah how few persons there are who understand practically the value of sufferings ! It is when Jesus visits us with the cross, that we are sure of being agreeable to Him. The Feet of Jesus nailed to that cruel Wood during three hours sufficed for the conversion of the universe ; these same Feet employed during three years in bearing in every direction, light and instruction, gained only five hundred disciples. It is not he who labors most for the glory of God, nor he that receives the most favors that is the holiest, but he who is the most crucified : witness the Blessed Virgin. To suffer in silence for Jesus, amidst crosses, anguish, and humiliations ;—Oh, that is being truly conformable to Jesus! There is nothing greater, holier or more to be desired."

So well did our beloved Mother St. Ursula understand and put in practice this doctrine, that it pleased the Almighty to bestow upon her the grace of a complete resignation to the will of God; a cheerful intrepidity in the view of her approaching dissolution; the exercise of a lively faith in the reception of the last sacraments; and, finally, a calm and peaceful exit from this world, in the firm assurance of a better.

Rev. Mother St. Ursula was the third Superior whose decease in that office had plunged the Community in grief. She was but sixty-one years of age, forty-five of which had been devoted to the service of God within the cloister.

REV. MOTHER MARIE-ANNE TASCHEREAU OF ST. FRANCIS XAVIER.

This venerable Mother, who was enjoying the repose of comparative obscurity, after guiding the Community twelve years, was elected again at the age of

seventy-one, to replace the much lamented
Mother St. Ursula. The following year
a *Golden Jubilee,* celebrating the half-
century's services of the " admirable
Mother," afforded the inmates of the
Monastery an opportunity of manifesting
their sentiments of love and gratitude,
leaving a pleasant an enduring souvenir
in the minds of all who shared the festivities.

But there are other memories to be
collected here around that beloved and
honored name, Mother Marie-Anne Louise
Taschereau of St. Fr. Xavier.

At the tender age of five, the little
daughter of the Hon. Thomas-Jacques
Taschereau, first crossed the threshold of
the Convent, her dark eyes sparkling with
joy as she glided from her loving mother's
arms to those of the good nuns. Holi-
days came often, and lasted long while
the little pupil was under ten years of
age. Then came the epoch of the first
Communion, when dolls and noisy games
are joyfully relinquished, for the sake of

the sweet, yet sublime lessons, contained
in that unpretending little volume, the
Catechism. The teachers of Mary-Anne
remarked, with delight, the unfolding of
the precious germs of future excellence,
as that young heart opened to the influence of grace under their careful guidance.

At the age of fifteen, Miss Taschereau
rejoined the family circle definitively. It
was the year of the Conquest. If the
gayeties of city-life were for a while banished from Quebec, they returned with the
first dawn of peace : and they were by no
means despised by our young lady.
During three or four years, she lost no
opportunity of sharing the pleasures the
world offers its votaries; yet, like many
others, failed to find in them the happiness they so loudly promise. The grace
of a special call to abandon the world,
was in reserve for her : it was heard during the exercises of the Novena of St.
François-Xavier, which, a century ago,
was celebrated in Quebec at the begin-

ning of Lent, with as much zeal, at least, as at the present day.

An eloquent preacher of the Society of Jesus, unfolding with lucidity the Sacred Text, many a sinner beat his breast with holy compunction; while among the just was heard the inquiry : " What shall I do to become more pleasing to God ? " One, at least, in that assembly heard in her heart the Saviour's answer, including the evangelical counsels of perfection : " Go, sell what thou hast and distribute thy goods to the poor : then, come and follow me that thou mayst have a great reward in Heaven."

Docile to the proffered grace, and fortified by the approbation of the Director of her conscience, Miss Taschereau seeks to execute her pious project with as little delay as possible.

A few weeks only after the Novena, all her preparations were accomplished. Regarding the monastery as the ark of her salvation, she quits the world and all she holds most dear, with a courageous heart and a holy intrepidity, which could only be inspired by the Holy Ghost.

" Never was there a more fervent candidate for the white veil. She desired to bear the name of St. Francis Xavier, having received the grace of her vocation through his intercession. From that moment, she adopted the great Apostle of the Indies as the model of her own ardor in the service of God. In ·these admirable dispositions she embraced all the practices of the religious life, and seemed to fly rather than to walk in the ways of perfection, advancing from virtue to virtue with undeviating perseverance. Naturally ardent and impetuous, her first attention was given to moderating her too great vivacity, and to acquiring the virtues of meekness and humility. By vigilance and prayer she soon obtained a complete victory over herself, thus rendering her soul most agreeable to the Celestial Bridegroom who had chosen her for his Spouse.

Mother St. Xavier was particularly

happy in forming to virtue the young
persons confided te her care for their
education. Her talents, as well as her
inclination, fitted her in a special manner
for the important charge of teacher; and
for many years her zeal found an ample
field for exertion in that department.

During thirty years, she occupied alternately the Office of Superior and *Dépositaire*.—In both she was a model which
her successors would esteem themselves
happy to imitate. As Superior, she was
zealous in preserving the primitive spirit
of simplicity, poverty, and retirement;
watchful to maintain the observance of
the Rule even in its minutest points;
attentive to procure the advancement of
each member of the Community in the
solid virtues of humility and charity.
Thus did our worthy Mother· St. Fr.
Xavier prove that her vocation was truly
from above; tending, as our Constitutions
demand, " *To the glory of God, the salvation of her own soul, and the good of the
Community.*"

At the age of eighty-two, this venerable
Mother was still one of the first to quit her
cell at the early hour of rising, and hasten
to cast herself at the foot of the Tabernacle in prayer. The crown of age rested
so lightly upon her brow, that it seemed
an ornament, rather than a burden ; and
the Community hoped to enjoy the precious advantage of her counsels and
example many years longer, when in
March, 1825, an epidemic cold laid her
prostrate ; and, in the space of a few days,
severing the tender ties that bound her
to her family of the cloister, she was reunited forever to that dearer home-circle
in heaven, where separations are unknown. [1]

[1] Rev. Mother St. Xavier's brother, the Hon. G.
E. Taschereau, Seignior of La Beauce—father of the
two Hon. Judges Taschereau, and grandfather of
Rt. Rev. E. A. Taschereau Archbishop of Quebec,
was a signal benefactor of the Ursulines by the care
he bestowed upon their temporal affairs.

CHAPTER XVII.

GRACE STRONGER THAN NATURE:

VOCATION OF THE MISSES BERTHELOT.

SUPERIORS.

The human heart is a spiritual battle-field, where grace and nature daily meet, and strive to obtain the mastery of that strong-hold, the will. Happy the soul that, watchful for the moment when the decisive blow is to be cast, calls on Heaven for succor, and assures her salvation by rendering grace victorious.

Such is the reflection that will naturally strike the reader's mind as it has our own, on witnessing the triumph of divine grace, in the vocation of the Misses Berthelot.

By the prominent position of their family in the city of Quebec, these young ladies were much exposed to be led away by the frivolous pleasures and vanities of the world.

Julia and her sister Teresa one year older than herself, were inseparable companions, whether in the Convent as school-girls, or in society ; moreover, in the family circle, the ties of nature and affection were knit so closely, the en- joyments were so real and each member seemed so necessary to the happiness of the others, that no thought of a separa- tion seemed admissible. The two sisters were certainly pious and edifying, yet they disdained neither the fashions, nor the gayeties of the world. One evening— or morning rather—as they were return- ing from a ball, their carriage drove past the Convent, just as the bell rang out its early call at four o'clock. The nuns were rising to offer to God the matin tribute of prayer and praise. Their souls were in peace. No idle regrets for baffled schemes of vanity : no aching remorse for stifling the voice of conscience, disturbed their serene content.

"Would to Heaven, thought Julia, that my own heart were as free and pure !" The carriage had paused at the door of

the rich merchant's aristocratic residence. The two young ladies alighted,
and mounted to their perfumed dressing-
room : but before retiring to rest, the
youngest of the two sisters had cast herself upon her knees, and offered herself
to God for a better purpose than had
hitherto engaged her thoughts.

A few days later, it was discovered
that Julia had serious thoughts of embracing the Religious life. For the first
time, the two sisters were of different
minds. Teresa could see nothing but
folly, in the project of renouncing the
world and immuring one's self in the
cloister. The " belle " of Quebec would
certainly not follow her sister's example,
nor throw aside her jewels, her lace, her
wreaths of flowers, for the robe of serge,
the band and veil of a nun. " Promise
me, Papa, she cries, that you will never
consent to see me a nun. Should I ever
be so infatuated as to desire it like my
sister Julia, do you at least, preserve me
from such madness."

Mr. Berthelot willingly gave his word ;

his own share in the sacrifice of his younger daughter, was quite enough he thought; and he knew the heavenly gates are not made to open exclusively on the inmates of a cloister.

The two sisters were together at the Convent-parlor when Julia demanded to be received among the daughters of St. Ursula. The nuns were loath to believe that either of the young ladies was destined for the Religious life. Both were dressed in the height of the fashion, in rustling silks, over which was worn an apron, or *over skirt*—as it would now be termed — of finest lawn, bordered with the costliest Valenciennes; their head-dress was interwoven with flowers that trembled on stems of silver and gold: their whole attire was of the utmost elegance.

Mother St. Clare, who was Superior at the time, (1789) not contenting herself with objections drawn from the obligation to give up one's will, to practice mortification, to live in poverty, and in conformity to the rule,—sought to try the vocation of the candidate by occular demonstration. Sending to the wash-room for one of the coarse hempen-aprons that are in use there, down to the present day, she displayed the article to her visitors, warning Miss Julia, that if she became a nun she would be required to wear a similar one, and to aid in the rough labor it seemed to typify. [1]

All this was not enough to alarm a generous heart. Julia entered the Noviniate leaving her sister to meditate on the wonders wrought by divine grace.

But another wonder was preparing. Like the youthful Gerard, who complained that his share was not equal to that of his brothers when they had aban-

[1] It is only of late years—since the labors of teaching have become multiplied—that the Choir-Nuns have ceased to aid in the wash-room. The writer of these pages remembers well having had her fingers belabored and bleeding by the over-generous use of the same wash-board, perhaps, that had served in the time of these ancient Mothers.

doned the whole paternal domain to him, choosing heaven for their portion, so Teresa felt herself in the wrong in preferring worldly pleasures to the service of God. The day came when repenting of the opposition she had shown to her sister's vocation, she was ready to beg on bended knees, that her father would forget the promise she had once exacted of him.

But Mr. Berthelot had not pledged his word, to release himself from it so easily. A whole twelve-month, Teresa expiated the rash precaution she had taken to prevent herself from being a nun. In aftertimes, she used to relate the story of her self-imposed troubles, always declaring that she only found the treatment she merited.

The two sisters, thus reunited after a brief separation, had the consolation of witnessing each other's progress in virtue, and enjoying each other's society in the House of God, during nearly forty years.

Mother St. Francis was slight and delicate in figure, naturally gentle, affable, and exquisitely polite. The full eulogium given by the Annalist, and the regrets of the Community, when a peaceful, happy death deprived the house of a useful and most edifying member, do not surprise us.

As to Mother St. Joseph, who was Superior from 1824 to 1827, and who lived till 1846, no one who knew her will fail to remember her as the type of the lady, — refined, amiable, and gentle in word and manner. "Her piety was accompanied by that simplicity which is the result of a child-like confidence in God, at the same time that it proved the calmness and innocence of her soul. Her favorite virtue was humility ; her constant aim, to conform herself to the will of others, revering in the voice of her Superiors that of God himself. In whatever office she was employed, she regarded herself as happy in fulfilling her duty for the glory of God and the good of souls."

It was during the superiority of Mother

St. Joseph (1826) that the Ursulines of
Quebec opened, with the recently established Convent of their Order in Waterford,
(Ireland) a correspondence which extended even to the pupils. It resulted in an
intimate interchange of good offices; a
union of heart and purpose, which have
been a source of mutual edification, and
reciprocal interest during half a century;
and which, we trust, will continue, with
all its advantages, as long as our two
Communities exist.

" During the last two years of her life,
this dear Mother seemed to have death
ever before her eyes.. In the conviction
of her approaching end, she redoubled
her fervor and her austerities, seeking
occasion to impose upon herself new sacrifices. She was preparing to celebrate
her golden Jubilee, which would occur on
the 2d of February, when, about a month
previous, she fell ill of the typhoid fever.
A few days of suffering, borne with exemplary patience, sufficed to break the
attenuated thread of life, opening to her
pure soul the possession of that Eternal

Good for which she had long labored and
sighed. It was on the 5th of January 1842."

The dear Waterford Nuns could only
be warned, by the spring vessels, that
our much esteemed Mother St. Joseph
was no more. In the mean time, in order
to celebrate the GOLDEN JUBILEE truly
in the Lord, these affectionate Sisters
had asked for general Communions, in
the intention of the venerated Ursuline
of Quebec, in all the Convents of Ireland ;
—Ursulines, Sisters of Mercy, and others :
they had begged the prayers of the
Jesuits, Trappists, Lazarists, and Brothers
of the Christian Doctrine. In their own
Community there were rejoicings, vows
and prayers, in accordance with the
warmth of their true, Irish hearts. It was
a strange contrast to the month's *Requiem*
in Quebec ; yet, how beautiful in the sight
of God, who is above all the GOD OF
CHARITY. Our pious Annalist expresses
the hope that the dear Mother, for whom
this mingled concert of mourning and
rejoicing met from the two borders of
the Atlantic, "contemplated the scene

from her throne in heaven; while we adore in silence the dispensations of Divine Providence, regulating all things for the good of the elect."

Mother St. Joseph had been the Secretary of Chapter, from 1823 to 1841 ; the last lines she traced in the Annals of the Monastery, were written within a few weeks of her death.

Having mentioned Mother Berthelot of St. Joseph in the capacity of Superior, as well as that of Annalist, let us not separate her from her successor in both offices, Mother Marguerite Boissonnault of St. Monica. A native of the parish of St. Valier (near Quebec), it was as a casual visitor that Miss Boissonnault first became acquainted with the Ursulines, to whose labors she was associated in 1813.

Doubtless, it was a great surprise to herself when, only twelve years after her profession, she was called to exercise the charge of Superior. Mother St. Monica was not, however, blessed with health : she was often a sufferer, but edified her

Sisters at all times, by her patience and resignation, as well as by her regularity, her zeal for the glory of God and the salvation of souls. It was one of her greatest consolations to be able to render service to youth by teaching, particularly in the department of the Extern-School, where she presided many years as general-mistress. Another ardent wish of her heart was gratified in seeing several members of her family called to consecrate their lives to God, in the Religious or in the Ecclesiastical state [1]. A great veneration for the traditions of the house and the *heroic times* of Canada, her country, a spirit of research joined to a taste for history, supplied the

---

[1] Rev. L. Ed. Bois, the worthy pastor who has labored with so much zeal during the past thirty-five years in the parish of Maskinongé, is a nephew of our deceased Mother St. Monica. The real services he has rendered his country by his excellent historical writings, may be traced to a bent of mind similar to that we have noticed above, in his esteemed relative. Two of Mr. Bois's Sisters embraced the religious state, in the Ursuline Convent of Three Rivers.

want of a regular course of studies, and
furnished Mother St. Monica with a fund
of information both useful and entertain-
ing. Notwithstanding her delicate health,
our venerated Mother lived to attain the
seventy-third year of her age, of which
she had devoted fifty to the service of
God in religion.

CHAPTER XVIII.

TIIE URSULINES OF THREE RIVERS, GUESTS OF THEIR SISTERS OF QUEBEC.

1806–1808.

On the 14th of October, 1806, at the
unwonted hour of nine o'clock in the
evening, the conventual door of the Monastery opened most willingly, to admit
sixteen Ursulines from Three-Rivers.

Shivering with the cold, weary and
benighted how welcome was the aspect

of the cloister !—doubly welcome at this
moment, by its contrast with the dis-
comforts of that small vessel in which
they had been tossed during four days.
How touchingly it reminded them of
their own dear retreat, from which the
pitiless flames had lately driven them !
Still more affecting was the sympathy,
betraying itself in tears, the tender embrace, the cordial, sisterly reception that
awaited them !

The hour was late for the Convent ;
but quickly the news had circulated
from cell to cell as if by the electric-
wires, and Sister after Sister gathered in ;
for how could they delay till morning to
testify their joy at such a meeting,—and
their grief at its cause ? Quickly the
hospitable fires, rekindled, brought the
steaming tea-urn, the restoring evening
repast ; while the low murmur of scarcely audible, yet animated conversation,
showed that the law of silence may sometimes yield—in a deferential way—to the
superior law of charity.

The conflagration of the Monastery of Three Rivers had taken place a month previous, yet how many details remained to be made known. Dear Reader, you have not failed to witness one of those too frequent, and ever heart-rending scenes!—the fire seizing upon the peaceful dwelling of a happy family; the belching smoke, the hurried issue of the frightened inmates; the din, the flames, the deafening shouts; the promiscuous gathering crowds! Such, and even more sad, had been the spectacle beheld at Three Rivers, on the 2nd of September.

With difficulty the Nuns and their boarders, with the poor sick people of the Hospital, avoided the awful fate that threatened them. The escape of all, under the circumstances, seemed almost miraculous. In less than an hour from the first alarm, the Convent, the Hospital, the Church, with roofs fallen in and crumbling walls, had been transformed to monuments of ruin and devastation.

Here were youth and age, the Nuns

and the objects of their care, to be sheltered and succored,—all driven at night-
fall from their happy asylum, and suddenly thrust upon the charity of the
public. The good people of Three Rivers,
for whom the affliction of the Nuns was
a family sorrow, and the burning of the
Monastery a real calamity, were not slow
to .manifest their sympathy and their
good will.

From every side were heard pressing
offers of shelter and hospitality ; but, as
the fire slackened, the Nuns perceived
that there still remained to them two
small buildings, the Extern school-house
and the bake-house. Within these narrow
limits, like our own Nuns on a similar
.occasion, they determined to reside, cling-
ing to the cloister like the bird to its
nest, even when the branch is severed
from the tree.

Although lodgings were found, there
was still sufficient room for the exercise
of charity. A Religious Community is a
large family to provide for, and some

among them were aged and infirm, beside the patients of the Hospital.

It was arranged, later, that a part of the Nuns should accept the invitation of their former Mothers of Quebec,—as we have seen.

Rev. Mother St. Olivier the Superior, with Mothers St. Croix, St. Angela, and Sr. St. Benedict a lay Sister, remained within the cloister, making a home of the bake-house where they managed to keep up a day-school, while the reconstruction of the Monastery was going on. The same narrow apartment served as a Chapel on Sundays for the Holy Sacrifice of the Mass. Such were the lodgings and accommodations of these generous nuns during thirteen months, at the end of which—November, 1807,—their new Monastery afforded them a welcome shelter.

Returning, now, to the guests so cordially welcomed at the Old Monastery, let us continue to observe the scene. Among them, our Nuns have recognized, here a relative, there an ancient pupil ; but above all others, one attracted their attention and tender compassion : this was an aged nun, so feeble and way-worn, that as she entered, she needed the supporting arm of her Sisters. It was Rev. Mother Theresa of Jesus (Ursule Baby) an ancient pupil, who by a singular destiny, after spending fifty-five years in the Monastery of Three-Rivers, and governing it as Superior, was now coming to end her days among her former Mothers, the Ursulines of Quebec.

She was returning to them, like a long absent wanderer to the home of his youth ; to find the friends of former days departed ; many old familiar haunts changed or faded from memory. Not one of the dearly beloved teachers of her childhood, remained to embrace her. Mother Davanne of St. Louis de Gonzague, had survived till lately ; but she, too, was gone, and she was the last of those olden times — "before the Conquest." Two of the oldest nuns, Mother Brassard of St. Magdalen, and Mother Cureux of St. Agathe,

both in their seventieth year, may have
met her a boarder, but they could scarcely claim the title of old schoolmates.

Mother Theresa of Jesus was already
looking forward to meet her former
friends in heaven, without a long delay.
She had not found them among the living;
but she had come to mingle her ashes
with theirs in the tomb.

It was a precious occasion for our Nuns
to surround the dying bed of their venerated Sister with all the soothing care that
kindness can imagine, or charity bestow.
The patient sufferer, as edifying as she
was beloved, lingered but a few weeks,
and after receiving the last consolations
of our holy religion, gently passed to a
better life, on the 14th of November, amid
the united prayers and regrets of the two
Communities. The Office for the dead,
the Burial Service, the last look at the
beloved and honored remains, the lowering of the coffin into the vault, sealed a
second compact of union and affection
between the two Houses,—while the first

yet subsisted in full force. Two of the
Sisters were recalled in January to aid
the little band in Three Rivers. The
remaining thirteen continued a whole
year more, with their Mothers of Quebec,
where they felt as much at home as if
they had always formed a part of the
Community.

At the end of fifteen months a new
Convent stood in place of that destroyed
by the fire. The letter that announced
the structure as completed, recalled the
Sisters from Quebec. A winter's journey
of five days in covered sleighs, took the
exiles home, one band in January, the
other in February 1808.

" The separation, says our Annalist, was
not effected without many tears on both
sides.".

The Ursulines of Three Rivers might
well bless the kind hand of Providence
for the restoration of their Monastery and
hospital; it was a munificent gift to receive from the liberality of friends. Their
chief benefactor on this occasion was

Bishop Plessis who took upon himself the responsibility of directing the work, and bringing it to a happy conclusion, generously supplying whatever was wanting in the funds furnished by the government and by the public.

According to the estimation of the eminent Prelate " The accident of the conflagration was permitted to show that the resources of Divine Providence are boundless, and to afford the faithful of the Diocese the occasion to manifest their charity, and testify their gratitude for the invaluable services the Ursulines have rendered all classes of society."

Our readers must be aware that prosperity has not ceased to shine upon that excellent Community down to the present day. The spacious and commodious buildings erected in 1808, have received several important additions, according to the increasing wants [1] ; for in Three Rivers as in the other parts of Canada, an awakened interest in the cause of Edu-

[1] The Community of Three Rivers is actually

cation has been promptly met by the cor-
responding zeal of Educational Establishments. Successive additions to the Convent buildings, of late years, have enabled
our Sister-Ursulines to offer every desirable accommodation to their numerous
pupils, proving that their zeal as Ursulines
does not suffer from being united to that
of genuine *Hospitalières.*

The only loss, beyond repair, inflicted
on the Monastery of Three Rivers by two
conflagrations, is that of their archives;
those precious documents which, had
they been preserved, would have enabled
the Nuns to reciprocate the offering, we
are happy to make them, of a history of
the early times in the Convent.

(1876) composed of 64 professed nuns, 40 of whom
are choir-nuns;—Novices, nine.

Pupils, including Boarders and Half-Boarders, 150:
Externs, 190.

For other particulars see Appendix, E.

CHAPTER XIX.

REV. MOTHER McLOUGHLIN OF ST. HENRY, SUPERIOR; MOTHER DOUGHERTY OF ST. AUGUSTIN :—

PIONEERS OF ENGLISH EDUCATION IN THE CONVENT.

1800-1846.

With the dawn of the XIXth century, the Thistle and the Shamrock entwine for the first time with the Fleur-de-lis and the Maple-Leaf, beneath the sheltering roof of the Old Monastery — the year 1800 presenting us as candidates for Religious profession, Mothers Mary-Louisa McLoughlin of St. Henry and Elizabeth Dougherty of St. Augustin, whose lineage shows both Scotch and Irish names.

Henceforth, the blooming garland, intermingled more or less with the Rose, in some of its varieties, will not cease to glow within the sacred shrine of St. Ursula, the divers leaves and flowers clasping in such close embrace, that to part them would be to destroy.

In the two worthy Mothers above-named, we have the pioneers of English education in the Convent. Directed hither, as if to answer the requirements of the epoch, furnishing the " right person at the right time," their vocation affords another instance of the admirable protection of Divine Providence over certain chosen souls, as well as over the Monastery.

Born in the same year, 1780, Miss Dougherty, in the city of New York, Miss McLoughlin at *Rivière du Loup* (below Quebec); deprived, till the age of fifteen, by the peculiar circumstances in which they were placed, of the inestimable happiness of making their first Communion, they met in the Ursuline Convent to perform that great act; and, at the age of twenty, pronounced the vows of Religion before the same altar, in the year 1800.

The talents of both were of a superior order, and the facilities afforded each for

the cultivation of her mind, were altogether peculiar, and seem really providential, when viewed in relation to the
duties that awaited them as Ursulines.

Miss Elizabeth Dougherty had been
tenderly and piously cared for, from her
infancy, by her mother, who was a native
of the city of New York, and a Protestant.
At the age of eleven or twelve, she had
visited London and Paris, in company
with her parents; and her voyage had
not been lost upon her, whether for the
information of her mind, or the polish of
her manners. Bereaved of his wife shortly after his return from Europe, Mr.
Dougherty had solaced himself with the
society of his little daughter, continuing
her studies in grammar, history, arithmetic and geography;—from these to astronomy—from earth to the skies—the
transition is natural. The rudiments of
French and Latin were a necessity, according to his views; for his own education was classical, and his tastes literary:
—they had been the cause of his volun-

tary exile from his native land, where the penal laws suffered no Catholic to rise above the soil on which he trod.

What particular motive had led Mr. Dougherty to come to Quebec, is not explained; in all probability it was the same that had driven him from New York to travel during the first years of the Republic ; the desire to preserve the allegiance he had sworn as a British subject.

The position that he occupied appears to have been that of an office-holder under the local government: Miss Elizabeth was at once placed under the care of the Ursulines. The course of religious instruction in preparation for her first Communion, made a profound impression upon her; for she was of an age to appreciate more fully than a child of ten or eleven, the sublime favor to which she aspired. From this period she dated her first attraction to the Religious state. The vivid sense of her immense obligations to Heaven, the firm determination to observe her baptismal vows, and to preserve the white robe of innocence bestowed anew in the Sacraments she had just received, inspired her with the utmost contempt of the world, and an ardent desire to give herself all to Him who had given himself to her as a pledge of eternal life.

At eighteen years of age, Miss Dougherty, who had spent three years in our classes, entered the Novitiate (1798), the mother-mistress being Mother Davanne of St. Louis de Gonzague.

Another young lady, Miss Mary-Louisa McLoughlin, as we have said, although born of Catholic parents living in Canada, had also deferred her first Communion till she was fifteen years of age. She was a grand-niece of that Col. S. Fraser, who commanded the Regiment of Scotch Highlanders at the taking of Quebec in 1759. Our readers perceive that already the Convent is winning members from the ranks of the *Conquerors*. John-Malcolm Fraser, brother of the Colonel, had married twice, and the daughters of his second wife, who was a Catholic, followed the religion of their mother.

Mary-Louisa, the little grand-daughter, was six years old, when she first appeared in the house of the old soldier; he was so charmed with her infantile graces that he declared she should not return with her parents to *Rivière du Loup*, and, almost by force, retained her as his adopted child.

She would be the light of the household in his declining years, and inherit more largely than her family, in the property at Rivière du Loup, which belonged to him as a retired Officer of the British Army.

Mr. and Mrs. McLoughlin were not without solicitude for the faith of their child; especially when they found her, as she grew older, attending the Sunday services with her grand-father, and going to a Protestant school, instead of the Convent.

Although Mrs. Fraser profited of every opportunity to instruct the child in the Catholic religion, according to the earnest request of both father and mother, yet, it

must be allowed, it was not without great
peril to the faith in which she had been
baptized, that Miss McLoughlin grew up
without participating in the life-giving
Sacraments of the Church At length,
her own reflections convinced her that
she could no longer remain a mere specta-
tor of what others were doing "to gain
eternal life." She felt that Religion, that
vital question on which depends the fate
of an immortal soul, could not be treated
as a matter of taste, or fashion, or con-
venience. She was not too young to consider seriously the path before her.

On the one hand, she had relatives,
friends, and acquaintances, belonging to
the first ranks of society, who professed
the various creeds that had made their
appearance in the country. On the other
hand, she was fully convinced on that
fundamental point, the unerring teaching
of the Church of Christ against which
" The gates of hell shall never prevail." A
decision, in conformity to her convictions,
followed; after which, a course of religious

instruction,[1] prepared her for the great
act of professing the Catholic Faith.
This ceremony took place in the Chapel
of the Seminary of Quebec, in presence
of the Superior Rev. Mr. Gravé, V. G.,
and of the young lady's father, Mr. John
McLoughlin. Passing over in silence
the storm raised by the disappointed
Colonel on this occasion, we follow with
pleasure the footsteps of this predestined
soul, as she obeys the impulse of grace,
soliciting, first, permission to enter the
Convent as boarder; and later, when her
pious meditations have convinced her of
the will of Heaven in her regard, arming
herself with true Christian courage, in
order to execute a project capable of
drawing upon her family very serious
consequences, as far as regarded their

---

[1] Miss McLoughlin's instructor on this important
occasion was the noble French exile, the Abbé Philippe
Desjardins, at that time Chaplain of the Hotel-Dieu.
On his return to Paris, he was named Vicar-General.
He never lost sight of his interesting pupil, but corresponded with her by letter till within a few months
of his death, 1833.

temporal prosperity. This new resolve
was "to make her calling and election
sure," by embracing the Religious state.
Placing her trust in Him for whom alone
such sacrifices ought to be made, the
great step was taken, with the consent of
her parents—not less generous than their
daughter—while the irascible relative
was absent on a journey. His terrible
wrath was again appeased ;—and thus it
became an authenticated fact, that there
beat in the breast of the veteran of former
battles, a forgiving heart, capable of re-
lenting on proper occasions; incapable, at
least, of committing a manifest injustice,
by attempting to constrain that *free-will*
which it has pleased the Almighty to
bestow on his intelligent creatures.

The ceremony of Miss McLoughlin's
taking the veil, on the 27th of February
1798, was preceded by a rite, rarely reserved for such an occasion. The Bishop
was there to administer, first, the sacrament of Confirmation : thus the plenitude
of the gifts of the Holy Ghost inundated

her soul, at the important moment of her enlisting under the glorious banner of St. Ursula.

Two years later (1800), in the joy of a heart overflowing with gratitude and love, the two happy novices whom we have brought before our readers, consummated their sacrifice by pronouncing their final vows.

Here we behold the two English teachers, to whom were confided the first regular classes in that language. The time was past when English-speaking pupils were content to learn French only in the Convent; nor could the French pupils afford to be ignorant of English. Forty years had multiplied the English portion of the population of Quebec, and had given them schools of their own, to which the pupils of the Convent would have been readily admitted.

Mother St. Augustin and her companion, Mother McLoughlin of St. Henry, were prepared to make their classes interesting and profitable. The former, as we haye seen, had received lessons from her father; the latter was initiated into the popular sciences by her friend and father-in-God, l'Abbé Desjardins.

In Geography, the Terrestrial globe was displayed ; maps were shown and the pupils taught to copy them; gleams of general History and Astronomy lent their aid. Within the Novitiate, other teachers were forming, as if in the perspective of a wider course of studies; while Divine Providence was preparing to reinforce the staff of English teachers by the vocation of Miss Genevieve McKutcheon (M. St. Helen) and Miss Margaret Cuddy (M. St. Athanasius).

If the services of Mother St. Henry and Mother St. Augustin were chiefly required for teaching English, they were not less qualified for the French classes. In painting, drawing, and embroidery Mother St. Augustin excelled :—yet these external accomplishments were of little value in the esteem of either, compared with one moment of recollection and

prayer. To develop the religious sentiment—that sentiment which elevates the
soul while it enlarges the mind—was,
above all, the object these true Ursulines
had in view, in the care they bestowed
upon their pupils.

But the two novices who had met from
points so far distant, were not destined
to continue their career together many
years.

Employed exclusively in teaching, as
long as her health permitted, Mother·St.
Augustin was placed at the head of the
Novitiate, in 1812, as a comparative repose.
But already her days were numbered;
death had marked her for his victim, and
in the springtide of 1814, like some fair
fruit, ripe before its time, suddenly har-
vested by one rude blast, Mother St. Augustin, struck down by a violent malady,
found in the bosom of her God an early
reward for her pure and holy life. She
was but thirty-five years of age.

Of Mother St. Henry's piety, her energy,
her promptitude in obeying the voice of

duty, our readers have formed an opinion by what they have already seen of her. Not less remarkable was her alacrity in the observance of the Rule, her lightsome countenance being ever expressive of interior joy and cheerfulness. The message sent by her former tutor, the Abbé Desjardins, was well understood, when writing from Paris he advised "Sr. St. Augustin to try to prevent Sr. St. Henry from laughing!"

The day came, however, all too soon for her desires, when the cares that devolve upon those who are charged with the principal offices, may have moderated the buoyancy of her youthful spirits. Six years had not yet elapsed after her profession, when she was named mother-mistress, with the obligation of guiding others in the path in which she was herself walking with such fervor. Her days of repose were already past. From the Novitiate to the Depot, from the Depot to the charge of Superior, (1818) such were the offices that Mother St. Henry was to fill alternately, during more than

a quarter of a century. Her zeal for the
instruction of youth, her enlightened
views of education, her numerous friends
in the highest ranks of society, as well as
among the clergy, the concurrence of her
brothers, the Drs. McLoughlin—both de-
votedly attached to her—in all her plans,
and their generosity in sending her from
Paris where one of them resided, whatever
would be useful to her in the schools;—
these were some of the peculiar circumstances that rendered her administration
a blessing to the Community in the important labors assigned to her direction
as Superior. Bishop Plessis, who had received the episcopal consecration about
the same time as Mother St. Henry made
profession, seconded all her efforts to
introduce a wider course of studies, and
manifested, on every occasion, the highest esteem both for her and for the whole
Community.

If our readers are aware of what Bishop
Plessis was towards his clergy, among his
people, or in his intercourse with stran-

gers, they may form an opinion of what Mother St. Henry was in her Community, among the pupils, and the many strangers who called to see her at the parlor, or who obtained permission to visit the interior of the Monastery. [1]

It was often remarked, that the motherly kindness with which she greeted all who approached her, seemed to be still more tender when it was exerted towards strangers, or towards those who were in need of compassion or assistance.

In 1836, Rev. Mother St. Henry, completing the fourth term of her superiority, saw herself again placed at the Depot, and successively in the other chief offices where her experience could be made available to the Community. The end of her useful career was announced by a painful malady, which after affording occasion for the practice of every virtue, and the triumph of patience, was crowned by a peaceful and happy death on the 3d of July 1846.

[1] See note F in Appendix.

The following tribute to the memory of the dear deceased, appeared on the *Quebec Gazette.*

" Died, on Friday, the third instant, at the Convent of the Ursulines of Quebec, Rev. Mother St. Henry (Mary-Louisa McLoughlin), at the age of sixty six years. During the long period of forty-six years of religious profession, she filled at various times the office of Superior of the Community, with that rare talent, prudence, and justice which merited for her the highest confidence and esteem. She will be long and deeply regretted, not only by the citizens of Quebec, of every class and nationality, who have so often rendered homage to her virtues and fine qualities, but also by all those stran-gers who have had occasion to visit that estimable Institution, none of whom ever went away without expressing the high-est admiration for the noble manners and the interesting conversation of this amiable lady."

Numerous letters, written by her hand, have been preserved, furnishing undoubt-

ed proof of her capacity for business, and
of her mental culture, as well as of the rare
qualities of her heart. Among the mour-
ners who wept by her bedside at the
hour of separation, were her three nieces,
Mother Joséphine Michaud of St. Cecilia,
—long employed in teaching or in the
capacity of general-mistress, and now
Assistant;—Mother Marie Talbot of St.
Margaret, and Mother Emilie Dechène
of St Fr. Borgia: a sister of the latter had
preceded her Aunt to the tomb, after
being professed only four years.

Mother St. Henry's portrait is one of
the few we have the good fortune to
possess of our ancient Superiors. It is a
copy of one executed by an artist, at the
special request of Dr. McLoughlin. It is
so life-like that we who bear the original
impressed upon our hearts, may still imagine, as we pause before it in the Community-Hall, that we really meet again
those eyes ever beaming with charity;
and that we hear the mellow tones of
that voice so soothing and maternal, which
we loved so well.

Often has it been remarked of Mother St. Henry, that it was sufficient to have seen her once to remain impressed with the highest respect for her as a Religious, and at the same time attracted by the charm of her conversation, her presence, her manners, all denoting the accomplished lady whose mind was even superior to her exterior endowments.

CHAPTER XX.

SISTER-NOVICES OF MOTHER ST. HENRY AND ST. AUGUSTIN.

OTHER ENGLISH TEACHERS.

The Novitiate, in a Religious House, represents, in some degree, the family-circle. Presided by a Mother-Mistress, whose office is truly maternal, since to her is confided the trust of forming the character of her youthful charge, teaching them to walk in the narrow path of perfection, and preparing, each to become the Spouse of Christ ; composed of souls yet in the infancy of the spiritual life, whose daily growth in holiness is often rapid and clearly perceptible ;—mutual confidence, mutual edification, establish relations truly fraternal, and impart to Sister-Novices a family resemblance, which often lasts as long as their lives.

For this reason we love to bring before us from time to time, a group of those Mothers who have commenced their Religious career together, persuaded that when we have studied the character of one or two, we have in a measure, the portrait of the others. Hence, having dwelt at some length, on the memory of Mother McLoughlin of St. Henry and Mother Dougherty of St. Augustin, the briefest notice of their Sister-Novices must suffice.

The amiable *senior* of the Novitiate in the year 1800, was Mother Angélique La Ferrière of St. Mary, so well known in later times, whether as general mistress of

the Boarders, Assistant-Superior, or Mistress of Novices. How her name will
quicken the memory of many ladies, now
past the meridian of life, but with whom
gratitude for the good counsels, the kind
offices of *la chère Mère Ste. Marie*, is still as
" fresh as the morning dew on beds of
roses." It was only in 1847 that her sweet
smile was missed among us. A brief malady, which found her ready for the great
summons, but her Sisters ill-prepared to
part with her—and all was over ! The
friend, who had ever words of encouragement and consolation at her command ;
the zealous promoter of education and
improvement, whether in our classes, or
among her novices; the fervent Religious,
rich in all the virtues of her state : such
was the loss the community was called
to deplore.

Next in rank of profession is Mother
Elizabeth Blais of St. Monica, who, apparently, entered the House of God, only in
the hope of finding it speedily the Gate
of Heaven. Eight years sufficed to win,
in answer to her prayers, the possession

of the eternal crown; and it seemed wrong to weep for one who bade adieu to life without one sigh, one fear, or one regret.

Mother Louise Olivier of St. Paul, and Mother Margaret Coutant of St. Anne, gave their quarter of a century to the humble and laborious life of an Ursuline; they merited to be held in esteem for their charitable and edifying conversation. Both were rewarded for a holy life by a happy death in the course of the year 1826.

Mother Marie-Françoise Aubin of St. Anthony, Sister Novice with the two preceding, doubled their career, rejoining them in a better world in 1852; her truly religious spirit, rendered her at all times very dear to her Superiors, and to all her Community.

The twin Sisters, Marie-Louise, and Marie-Therese Oneille, bearing in religion the names of St. Gertrude and St. Catherine, were ever " burning and shining lights" by their angelic life.

It was in favor of the Irish class—the Externs—that the amiable Mother St. Catherine, put to profit the facility she had acquired in speaking English, and displayed an eloquence, a pathos, which many a sacred orator might envy. Her instructions doubtless owed their efficacity to that ardent love of God with which her heart was on fire : for, on these occasions, she seemed inspired. Her death, in 1842, preceded by an illness of only three days, filled the Convent with grief. So sudden a stroke found no one prepared, but the dear soul who so submissively accepted it, as the signal of her eternal happiness. The recitation of the Divine Office on that memorable 28th May, was nigh being interrupted ; and at the dinner hour, on the following day, no one could command her emotion sufficiently to read, during the meal, as is the custom.

Oh! how we pitied that other sister, Mother St. Gertrude, nor thought she could survive the separation. But, as some one has said, "grief does not break hearts." The tender ties of nature had been strengthened by forty years of their Religious life, spent together ; Death could not burst them asunder. One had merely gone before ; the other would wait the hour to follow ; and so she peacefully, silently bears her cross, and follows on in the narrow path as before. Ten years later (1852), that fragile frame, after undergoing long and severe sufferings, set free, at last, the willing, the pure, the blessed spirit—

> The choir of Virgins pure and bright,
> Around their Sister press'd ;
> And hymns of welcome sweet they sang
> " Come, weary one and rest ! "

Adverting again to the special consideration we had in view, in another chapter—the introduction of the English language into our course of studies,—we recall with pleasure the names of Mother St. Helen and St. Athanasius, who, after being the pupils of Mother St. Augustin in the Boarding School, became her novices in 1807. Many of our readers remember both of these ancient, venerated

Mothers, who, although of apparently delicate constitutions, attained the ages, respectively, of seventy-two and eighty-five, celebrating the one the fifty-first, the other the sixty-fourth year of her profession.

The merits of Mother St. Athanasius and her long labors are known, we might say, to all the Irish population of Quebec and its environs. She was born in Kilkenny, and came out to this country when but a child. Her father, who belonged to the military, died almost on their arrival. Kind friends provided for the widow and the child. Little Margaret was placed at the Convent, at the age of fourteen, by one who hoped that when she had grown up, he would be found to suit her choice. But the young girl took her decision in the calm of her heart, bestowing its affections on a heavenly Spouse. Sending for her protector, she informed him of her intention to ask admission among the daughters of St. Angela.

It is related that, waiving his claims in

a truly Christian spirit, the young Officer used neither reproach nor entreaty to dissuade the chosen one from following the call of Heaven. A few months later, in presence of "men and angels," Miss Cuddy proclaimed her intention of " persevering until the end of her life in bearing the sweet yoke of Jesus Christ," and exchanged her name for that of St. Athanasius, while she received the veil and vesture of an Ursuline. Thus, at sixteen, commenced a long and useful career of more than three-score years within the cloister. .

Possessing a ready memory, an ardent temperament, a warm *Irish* heart, she loved, next after God, her country, and all that belonged to the Green ISLE OF ERIN. To the latest day of her life, she remembered with vivid emotion, her native land.

Charged with the Irish children at the Extern-School from the time it was opened (1822), she spared neither labor nor pains to contribute to the spiritual and temporal welfare of all who came within her influence. As a teacher, she was indefatigable, holding the reins of government with a firm yet even hand. Her politeness was proverbial; and if good manners contribute in no small degree to the well-being of the family circle, and of society in general, in this respect also, the name of Mother St. Athanasius challenges a tribute of gratitude.

Our limits forbid us to dwell longer upon this amiable figure of our epoch; yet we omit with regret much that would charm and edify, both in the life of this venerable Nun, who has so recently left her place vacant among us (1875); and in that of Mother McKutcheon of St. Helen, whose name, even during her life-time, was esteemed synonymous with that of *Saint*. Long infirmities, borne with the patience of one who habitually contemplates the Crucifix, did not prevent her from discharging the duties of teacher, and especially that of mistress of novices, with notable success. An unction, as sweet as it was penetrating, pervaded her words, which ever made a deep impression, whether in simple conference with her novices, or in addressing collectively her little flock. It was in 1862, while the Community were engaged in the exercises of an annual retreat, that our beloved Mother St. Helen closed in peace her earthly career.

She, who had been the third English-speaking novice received in the Monastery, left twelve teachers of that language; yet not one too many for the ever increasing demands of the Institution.

CHAPTER XXI.

THE URSULINES OF QUEBEC AID THEIR SISTERS, THE URSULINES OF NEW ORLEANS, U. S.

1822.

In the days when New France extended from the Gulf of St. Lawrence, along the Mississippi, to the Gulf of Mexico, there were, at an early date, Ursulines at Quebec and at New Orleans,—the two extreme points of that vast empire. In 1727, French Nuns from Rouen, at the demand of the first missionary of those newly-discovered regions of the West, founded a Convent, which soon rendered the services that might have been required of three or four different Institutions.

Instruction for colored-women, a day school for children, a hospital, a house of refuge : such were the good works commenced by the Ursulines within three

years of their foundation. The terrible
massacre of the Natchez, which happened
soon after, gave them the melancholy occasion of opening a vast Orphanage. Thus
the foundresses of the Monastery of New-
Orleans, like those of Quebec, had a providential mission to accomplish, before
they entered upon the regular duties of
their primitive vocation.

From time to time, our Nuns had corresponded by letter with their Sister Ursulines, who had applied to them for aid.
It was not pecuniary aid that was solicited, the Convent being richly endowed ; but something more difficult to
obtain, and which, in Louisiana, was rarer
than money. That colony, so different
from Canada, both in its first settlers and
in the enervating effects of its climate,
offered little resource to recruit a Religious establishment. On the other hand,
Quebec, by the difficulty of communication, was further from New Orleans than
from Paris. " A year's journey, says Mother
St. Louis de Gonzague, is really too long

to be thought of. Were it a question of going to France, we might deliberate, but not to the Mississippi."

In 1821, Bishop Plessis received from Bishop Dubourg, to whom the diocese of New Orleans had lately been confided, a communication, exposing the necessities of that precious Institution, " so necessary to the welfare of his flock—now sorely tried, and in danger of perishing, if not succored in season." The Monastery counted nearly a century of existence, yet, as in the times when our own Mother Mary of the Incarnation and Mother St. Athanasius were asking help from France, the Community of New Orleans consisted of the aged and the young, without the intermediate link—the middle-aged, uniting the maturity and the experience necessary for the more important offices.

In the words of Bishop Dubourg;— "The ancient columns of the edifice were in a state of decay, and at the approaching moment of their fall, there would be found only feeble reeds to supply their

place." The demand was, therefore, for
" three or four professed nuns of mature
age, of good judgment, and formed to the
practice of virtue, to fill up the interval between the aged and the young " The
case was clear; but the prospect of giving
up several subjects, so precious to any
Community, was not inviting.

Further negotiations however, smooth-
ed the difficulties, and the following year
(1822), three candidates for the arduous
mission were named. They were Mothers
Félicité Borne of St. Charles, Angélique
Bougie of St. Louis de Gonzague, and Pélagie Morin of St. Etienne ; all between
thirty and forty years of age, and well
qualified for the difficult position that
awaited them.

The gratitude of the worthy Bishop,
and of the Ursulines of New Orleans, on
learning the happy issue of their appeal,
was without bounds. " A thousand blessings upon you, writes Bishop Dubourg
to Bishop Plessis, for the benevolent interest you have taken in the success of

my petition. Our Ursulines share my gratitude, both towards your Lordship, and towards their honored Sisters of Quebec. We shall receive the precious acquisition as a present from Heaven ; and as a new mark of that wonderful goodness of God which we have experienced so palpably for several years past."

The great decision being taken, preparations were made for the journey. It was quite an event, not only for the three good Mothers, the even tenor of whose life was so unexpectedly disturbed ; but for the wide circle of friends, relatives, and acquaintances, scattered through the length and breadth of the country.

The departure was definitively fixed for the 3d of October. On the 2d, Bishop Plessis came to the Convent to offer the Holy Mass, and give Communion to the generous missioners, happy to see them prepared to make their sacrifice with generosity. Rev. Father Maguire, then pastor of St. Michael's, had been chosen to be the Raphael of the voyage, preluding, by this signal service, to the many benefits he would have occasion later to bestow upon the Ursulines of Quebec. On the day of the departure, the touching prayers for voyagers in the Roman Itinerary, were recited after Mass with emotions not easy to describe : nor shall we attempt to tell how that last-day-at-home was passed !

At six o'clock the final adieu had been said ; a parting embrace had separated them whom mutual charity and a similar choice of Heaven, had united in the sacred bonds of religious friendship.

The three missioners, in travelling attire, pass the Conventual door, traverse the silent groups of sympathizing friends, enter the carriages that are waiting for them, and are conducted as in triumph to the wharf in Lower-Town. The steam-boat, lying at anchor and illuminated to honor the occasion, rested till an advanced hour of the evening, in order to allow the visits of friends to be prolonged.

At Three Rivers, another Ursuline,

Mother Normanville of St. Helen, was
waiting to offer a similar sacrifice, by
joining the missionary-band, thus completing the number of professed nuns
demanded. Capt. Morin, who seemed
to have placed his vessel entirely at the
disposition of the travellers, waited till
they had visited the Convent, and received the blessing of the venerated Abbé
de Calonne.

On Saturday, at four o'clock P. M.,
they were at Montreal. The quay was
crowded with people, willing to see those
Ursulines who were so courageously
exiling themselves for the love of God ;
but their prudent conductor, Rev. T.
Maguire, enabled them to avoid the gaze
of the curious :—Capt. Morin landed them
on a private wharf, within a few rods of
the Hotel-Dieu. The kindness of these
good Nuns, the cordial welcome of the
Sisters of the Congregation, and all the
affection that awaited them at the General Hospital, were described by our voyagers in grateful terms ; but pausing only

one day in Montreal they proceed to New
York, with an addition to their party of
three young ladies from Detroit, candidates also for the life of the cloister in the
South.

It was not a mere day's journey, at that
time, to go from Montreal to New-York.
Between La Prairie and Lake Champlain
our travellers had to endure the fatigue
of carriage-conveyance; thence by steam-
boat, amid " passengers of every color,
and almost every nation," they reach the
great City, on the 11th October, the fifth
day after leaving Montreal.

Happy were the tired voyagers to receive hospitality at the hands of the Sisters of Charity, recently founded in the
United States by that admirable woman,
Mother Seton.

On the 21st October, Rev. Th. Maguire
resigned his post as conductor of the
missionary band, in favor of Rev. Mr.
Janvier, a worthy priest deputed by
Bishop Dubourg to this effect; and the

whole company embarked for a sea-voyage of twenty days.

More adventures than pleasures were in store for them. They had not been a week out at sea, when the most oppressive heat they had ever experienced, gave them a foretaste of the zone they were approaching. Then a furious storm came on, during which a sailor was swept overboard. In attempting to rescue the unfortunate man, the vessel was for a moment on the point of being submerged; the waves came dashing over the deck inundating the passengers' rooms, and, but for a skilful manœuvre, a watery grave might have been the end of the voyage. But this was nothing in comparison with the peril of an encounter with pirates. Happily, the Captain perceived the ship in season not to be the first attacked. The thirty men-passengers on board were armed, and ordered on deck to aid the mariners; their seven guns were charged, and a vigorous fire soon forced the pirates to draw off. As the enemy disappeared, the Packet-Ship spread her sails, and soon regained the time lost.

The terror of our poor nuns may easily be conceived ; but as no harm befell them, they had only to change their petitions for the protection of Heaven into thanksgivings, the danger being over.

A false rumor, however, gave their friends in Canada more than six weeks of cruel suspense and anxiety. The report was that the pirates had captured the Packet-Ship and made the crew prisoners, retaining their prize twenty-four hours, when another vessel, the *Alligator*, had attacked the pirates and forced them to give up their booty. Such a catastrophe was commented upon and deplored on every side ; there was no end of conjectures and visits of condolence. It was only on the 2d of January that letters from our nuns, furnished a correct account of the affair. This was promptly published on the *Canadien*, in order to relieve the anxiety of the many friends interested in the fate of the voyagers.

In the mean time, our Ursulines had reached their destination. The venerable Superior, Mother St. Michael, who had been inspired to ask for them, had only waited,—it would seem—to hear that her request was granted, in order to die contented, in the assurance that her dear Community would be well provided for. Her successor wrote, with a gratitude most touching, her thanks for " the precious boon ; praying that the Almighty might preserve the dear Sisters long, for the salvation of so many souls who, without the instruction given in the Convent, would never know God."

The generous exiles, on their part, were not disappointed in their new Sisters ; the kindness with which they were greeted on arriving, was but one instance of the charity that reigned supreme in the Convent, and which ever surrounded them with its ineffable charms.

In 1824, the Ursulines of New Orleans exchanged their ancient Convent in the City, for a more salubrious site, at the di

tance of about two miles, where they
built their present Monastery—a spacious
brick edifice two hundred feet long, with
two wings in the rear.

Our Sisters continued to render impor-
tant services to their adopted Commu-
nity till called to their reward,—Mother
St. Louis de Gonzague in 1833, Mother
St. Etienne in 1846. One was still living,
in 1849, to welcome and encourage two
other members of the Monastery of
Quebec—Mothers Victoria White of St.
Jane-Frances de Chantal, and Catherine
Burke of St. Thomas, [1] who had gene-

[1] Mother J. F. de Chantal labored nineteen years
in the South, and only returned to the "Old Monastery" after seeing the two new foundations of Galveston and San-Antonio,—both of which she had
governed as Superior—in the way of prosperity.

Mother St. Thomas, on whom the climate preyed
severely, demanded her recall after rendering important services in Galveston during six years.
Many of our readers are aware that a "providential
mission" awaited her at home, and the Histoire des
Ursulines is there to attest with what filial affection
she cherishes the Old Monastery of Quebec. The

rously accepted an invitation to aid the newly-founded Convent of Ursulines in Galveston, Texas.

Although Mother St. Charles—the latest survivor—always suffered from the climate of New-Orleans, so different from that of her native land, still her vigorous constitution bore her to the advanced age of sixty-nine years, thirty of which she had passed in the South.

The triple link between the two oldest Communities of Ursulines in America, was strengthened again, in 1836, when, through the mysterious decrees of Divine Providence, the devoted little band of Ursulines, driven from their Convent on Mt. Benedict [1] (Charlestown, Mass.) took refuge with the various Communities of their Order; two remaining with the Ursulines of Quebec, two others joining the

Glimpses acknowledges, with pleasure, its obligations to the patient and persevering researches made by Mother St. Thomas.

[1] See Appendix G.

Ursulines of Three Rivers, while three offered themselves to the Convent of New Orleans. The important services these sorely-tried Religious were enabled to render, in each of these their adopted Communities, must have served to console them, and gradually to efface the remembrance of the disaster, with the hope long-nourished of seeing it repaired.

CHAPTER XXII.

EDUCATION IN OUR CONVENT-SCHOOLS IN THE PRESENT CENTURY.

Catholic Institutions for education in Canada, had found in the policy of the government inaugurated in 1759, difficulties to which we have briefly alluded elsewhere. At the beginning of the present century, these Institutions were far from the high position which they have at last attained throughout the land.

Within the cloister, as well as among the mass of the population, the scale of instruction had evidently descended.

It would be an interesting study, to trace the gradual rise of our Convent-teaching, from that simple, yet fundamental course;—Christian Doctrine, comprising sacred history; reading; writing; arithmetic, and needle-work,—to which it was mostly confined seventy or eighty years ago, to the wider circle it embraces at the present day.

By comparing the notes furnished by our Annals, it is evident that the impetus given to studies about the year 1800, both in the novitiate and in the classes, by the well-directed efforts of Mothers St. Henry and St. Augustin, was but the first wave of a new and powerful current, which without tearing up the solid bed of a time-worn channel, began to flow more swiftly, imparting fresh verdure and plentiful flowers along its pleasant banks.

Already in 1810 " pupils commenced to be more numerous, and to remain longer at school." In 1815, Bishop J. O. Plessis regulated " that more time should be allotted to the studies of the Novices, in order to render them proficient in the various branches which they were required to teach, French and English Grammar, Geography, &c. " These branches, adds the Annalist, attract pupils to the Convent, and afford us an opportunity to form them to the virtues of a Christian life."

Half-Boarders had been admitted from the year 1800. Their class-rooms were distinct from those of the boarders until 1825, when the two schools were united, in order to afford greater facility for grading the classes, " according to the rule." To the new branches already introduced, were added History and Translation.

The number of Boarders varied from sixty to eighty : the Half-Boarders were in greater number.

The Extern-School had never ceased to be numerous. In 1822, Rev. J. Signay, charged with the parish of Quebec, applied to the Ursulines to obtain instruction for the Irish Catholics of the City. We may judge what zeal animated our Mothers of that period, by the fact of their receiving sixty of these young girls immediately, although they were obliged to admit them during the hours that the French pupils were absent, from eleven o'clock to one, in order to have class-rooms. Many of these children being very poor, had to be supplied with the nourishment of the body, as well as that of the soul.

The Irish Class was definitively organized, and opened to the scholars at the same hours as the French Canadians, in ·1824. Between seventy and eighty children assembled, at once, to receive elementary instruction in English, under the devoted superintendence of Mother St. Athanasius, whose name has become a household-word with the Irish, for her long and laborious services in the Extern-School.

While our nuns were thus imposing upon themselves new labors, a wider and higher course of studies, in the solid, as well as in the ornamental branches, was being elaborated.

Mother Dougherty of St. Augustin had formed excellent pupils, especially in drawing ; among these Mother Julie Painchaud of St. Borgia, rivalled and even surpassed her teacher. During the eighteen years of her too brief career, she was employed exclusively in the Boarding-School, where she succeeded no less in forming her youthful charge to piety and good manners, than in cultivating their talents and ornamenting their minds.

To descend to particulars, we should state here, that the first lessons in crayon and in oil-painting were received from a French artist in 1820. Twelve years later, Mr. Bowman, a painter of distinction from Boston, was called in to cultivate the talents of our young *artists*, and with such success that the principal altars and shrines within the Monastery, were soon decorated with paintings due to their skill. One of the best qualified in that class of painters, Miss Emilie Dechêne, entered the Novitiate later, to dedicate her talents to the service of the Convent;— nor has there been wanting, down to the present time a lineal succession of artists, inheriting the talents, and benefited by the labors of their predecessors.

Musical instruments were not unknown, in some of their simpler forms, even in the early times of the Convent. The piano-forte was introduced by a friend of the Convent, Mr. J. B. Glack-meyer. Regular lessons were first given to the pupils by Mr. Codman, the organist of the Anglican Cathedral. In 1824, there were novices qualified to give music-lessons, and some ten years later, secular teachers were no longer required for any instrument, the organ, harp, and guitar included.

The next fifteen years presented a concurrence of circumstances singularly favorable to the complete development of a high course of studies.

First, the awakening, in the Country,

of a new interest in the cause of education : a Society under the sanction of the
Governor and approved by the Bishop,
to further that cause—first organized in
1820 —becoming every day more popular,
and acquiring new importance.

Secondly, as regards, more directly, the
Convent : able and energetic Superiors,
both ecclesiastical and local ; devoted
friends among the Clergy, particularly
the Priests of the Seminary (Quebec) ; accomplished teachers, among whom we
must specify, in addition to those already
mentioned, Mother Cecilia O'Conway of
the Incarnation, who, from being a Sister
of Charity in New York, became an Ursuline, joining our Community in 1823.

Carefully educated by her father, who
was a linguist and a man of extensive
learning, Mother Cecilia of the Incarnation had acquired also a fund of useful
information by experience, before giving
her services to the Monastery of the Ursulines. To a natural taste for those
sciences which in our century have be-

come so popular, Botany, Physics, Mineralogy, &c., she joined uncommon skill in all the varieties of fancy-work and embroidery. Active and energetic, she possessed all that love for teaching, that sympathy for her pupils, that zeal for their progress, so necessary to form a successful instructor.

About the same date, opened an intimate and cordial intercourse by letter with the Ursuline Convent, St. Mary's, Waterford (Ireland), recently founded by the Ursulines of Cork.

Through the kindness of these highly educated Sister-Ursulines, the Classes were furnished with excellent treatises and models of literature in English; specimens in Natural History; and curiosities, sufficient to form the germ of a Museum, which every year has augmented down to the present day.

In 1831, commenced that series of modern improvements, by additions to the original buildings, which have continued, from time to time, during almost a halfcentnry. A new story, added to the main-building, gave two large halls, and four smaller class-rooms for the better accommodation of the boarders. These were blessed with solemnity, and with pious rejoicings on the 15th of Oct., 1832, by Bishop Signay. After the ceremony, Lady Aylmer, without the Governor, and attended only by the ladies of her suite, paid a gracious visit to the pupils in their new class-rooms. The same day, other ladies of the city, the parents and relatives of the pupils, enjoyed also that rare privilege of viewing the interior of the Monastery, permission having been given to that effect.

The appointment of Rev. Th. Maguire as chaplain, won for the Convent the services of that eminent friend of education, for the consolidation of the new plan of studies, and the spiritual direction of the Community. A voyage to Europe (1834–36) afforded an opportunity to visit various educational Institutions, and to purchase instruments, with stores of curiosities, books, &c., for the Ursulines, to whose interests he was devoting himself during the nineteen remaining years of his life.

Returning to Canada by the way of New-York, in 1835, our Rev. Father was requested by the Bishop of Boston to be the conductor of the remaining members of the Convent of Charlestown (Mass.), a part of whom had already sought protection in the Old Monastery of Quebec. [1] Driven from their peaceful asylum at midnight, August 13th 1834, by a heartless, deluded mob, they had failed in obtaining redress at the hands of Justice, seated in the tribunals of Massachusetts, and they were now, though with reluctance, abandoning the work of benevolence to which they had desired to consecrate their lives.

When the final arrangements had been made, permitting the Ursuline Convents of Three Rivers and New Orleans, to share the services of these worthy Religious, two of them gratefully accepted

[1] Appendix H.

the dispositions of Divine Providence which assigned to them, as their future home, the House founded by Ven. Mother Mary of the Incarnation.

Thus were acquired the services of Mother Elizabeth Harrison of St. Joseph, an excellent Religious, and a musician in the style of Saint Cecilia, under whose thrilling touch,

...... The pealing organ swelled,
Filling the soul with thoughts divine.

Mother Mary Barber of St. Benedict personified as well the Three Graces, who in her were not only Christian, but eminently religious. By Mother St. Benedict, the teaching of the English language, already thoroughly domiciliated within the Monastery, was placed on the same basis as the French—a standard which it has never since ceased to maintain. Thus admirably has it pleased Divine Providence to dispose of all events, and crown with blessings a House dedicated to the greater glory of God and the salvation of souls.

Among the motives of encouragement, and the stimulants to exertion in the cause of Education, during the years under our consideration, justice, as well as gratitude would lead us to mention the high patronage, the friendliness and good will of the Governors of Canada and their noble families. At all times, a visit of a new Governor to the Ursuline Convent, has seemed to follow as naturally his arrival, as any · another ceremony of his installation. The New-Year's-visit to the Ursuline Convent, was as much a rule of etiquette at the Castle, as the New-Year's ball, offered to the citizens.

More frequent and more intimate were the visits of Her Ladyship and the children. Lady Provost and her daughter, the Countess Dalhousie, Lady Aylmer, were personal friends of the Nuns,—seeking occasions to enjoy their society, taking interest in the amusements of the pupils, or their success in their studies. More than once, some present of value in teaching, —a chart, a rare print or drawing, &c.,

would follow the examination of a class, where one of these kind Ladies presided. Lady Aylmer's friendly visits (1830-34) in the class-rooms, and the emulation they excited will never be forgotten. [1]

In our own days, what delightful affability on the part of a Lady Elgin, a Lady Head, in their intercourse with the Ursulines! How charming, how gracious the visits of a Lady Monck, a Countess Dufferin! what cordiality on the part of an ancient pupil, a Lady Belleau, a Lady Caron! how precious the prizes awarded at their hands, or the wreath they have placed upon the brow of a happy gra-

---

[1] " In April 1831, *Milady Aylmer*—writes the Annalist—accompanied by several ladies of the City, honored our boarders so far as to assist at the examination of the higher classes, and expressed herself as extremely satisfied with their answers. The examination lasted three hours. Her Ladyship had the goodness to present crowns of roses to the two that had most distinguished themselves, and to bestow the Cross of St. Louis upon two others for their application:—the cross was worn several days, according to our custom at these examinations."

duate, at the public Session that closes the scholastic year. But we are anticipating.

In turn with the presence of the Governor, or the Lady of the Castle, it was the annual, or the occasional visit of the chief Pastor of the diocese that awakened new zeal, and encouraged to new efforts for the good cause.

Let our readers judge of this by an extract from a letter, addressed to the Community by Rev. P.-F. Turgeon, [1] charged by Bishop Signay with the direction of the Monastery. "Since several years—writes the new Superior in 1833—your Educational department has acquired an importance, highly gratifying to all the friends of Religion. The efforts you have made to place your boarding-school on the respectable footing it now occupies, are viewed with admiration. All classes of society rejoice to see, that in addition to the good education you gave heretofore, you have introduced several branches, which, although they may not be of great

[1] Later, Bishop of Quebec.

practical utility, have one great advantage, that of enabling young girls to complete their education in a pious asylum where their religious instruction will ever be kept in view. Pious mothers esteem themselves happy to be exempted from the necessity of placing in profane hands the treasures they confide to yours without anxiety.

" I feel a lively satisfaction in perceiving that piety and virtue distinguish the pupils of your Institution etc."

Another appreciation of the education given forty years ago in the Convent, may not be uninteresting. We shall take it from the Newspaper account of a visit to the Ursulines, altogether unprecedented.[1] The great Hall, *St. Ursula*, had been prepared for the occasion, as well as the pupils; for a little dramatic entertainment was to constitute the *reception* given to the most august assembly that Quebec could afford. The Rt. Rev. J. Signay,

---

[1] See Appendix I.

Bishop of Quebec, attended by several members of the Clergy, and a large number of lay gentlemen, some of whom were hoary with age, while all were most respectable by their character and position, had been introduced within the cloister, on the 14th of January, 1836. On the following day appeared on the *Canadian* [1] the subjoined account :—

" Yesterday afternoon, the Hon. Speaker and members of the Legislature, were admitted to visit the Ursuline Convent of this City. The pupils of the Institution represented, in presence of this honorable company, a Sacred Drama, which alone would suffice to give the highest idea of the classical education young ladies receive in this pious Institution. Specimens of painting, drawing, and needlework, in all their varieties, which these gentlemen had an opportunity to examine, raised their admiration to the highest degree : and all were enchanted with the grace of the pupils, as well as

[1] Editor, Et. Parent, Esq.

the affability of the ladies to whose zealous and enlightened care they are confided."

The culminating point, as regards the efforts made in Canada to encourage education and render it popular, was the introduction of public Examinations. The experiment had been tried at the Seminary-college of Quebec in 1830, and the following years, with full success. In 1837, the pupils of the Ursulines, for the first time, presented themselves before an audience assembled at the invitation of their Convent Mothers, to be examined on the different branches they had studied.

It was on the 31st of January. Rev. Father Th. Maguire had offered "the chaplain's room" — not more spacious at that time than at the present day—for the occasion. At one side was the Bishop's *fauteuil*, with chairs for some twenty priests who had been invited. The other extremity of the apartment was arranged for a class of young ladies : Maps and the Globes; the black-board for the Grammar-

class, for Arithmetic and tracing maps;
Composition books, written by the pupils;
specimens of their Painting, Drawing and
Embroidery, suspended along the walls.
There was also a piano for musical fingers;
the harp displayed its fine proportions;
·and guitars, their graceful forms. About
one hundred pupils were in readiness in
the adjoining apartments, to enter, one
class at a time, to be examined. The Pro-
. grammes and Question-lists on the various
branches, were in the hands of Rev. Father
Maguire, who invited, now, the Pastor of
Quebec, Rev. C. F. Baillargeon; now, Rev.
P. McMahon of St. Patrick's church; now
the Pastor of St. Roch's, or some other
Rev. gentleman, to test the proficiency of
the young students. The morning session
was from nine o'clock to eleven; the afternoon, from two to four o'clock, during
three successive days; the more serious
labor of the examination being diversified
by the occasional recitation of a fable, a
poem or a dialogue; by music and singing; or by the reading of an original composition.

At the opening of the last session, the apparatus of a school-room had disappeared. A king's throne, and tapestried walls, transported the spectators to a palace : it was that of Assuerus, the Assyrian monarch, as depicted by Racine in his Tragedy of Esther. The *Dramatis personæ* succeeded in fully interesting their auditory ; but they were in turn even more interested, it may be, themselves— and we write here from personal souvenirs—when the names of the successful competitors in the arena of science being proclaimed, they came forward to receive, at the hand of the good Bishop, the much-prized testimonial,—a wreath of flowers, or a book inscribed with their name. A valedictory address, a few words complimentary and encouraging from the venerated Prelate who had presided—and the Exercises of the Examination were over. They had passed off to the entire satisfaction of all parties concerned.

The following year, the large Hall in the new wing *Ste. Angèle* was opened to a similar audience : but another concession was now clamorously demanded. Parents were only half satisfied, to know that their daughters had done themselves credit by passing a good examination; they must witness it themselves:—no one had a better right. The question having been carried before competent authority, and decided in favor of the public, in 1839, the exercises took place in presence of the parents, guardians, and sisters of the pupils. The Bishop with the Clergy of the City, the Judges and other friends of Education, continued to form the "Board of Examiners" at the three sessions of Wednesday and Thursday (January 30th and 31st), which were held in the same large Hall that had been occupied the preceding year. The Mother Superior, and a certain number of the Nuns, from an adjoining apartment, could oversee the pupils as they presented themselves before the audience, and superintend the proceedings.

The programme of the Examination, of which we here subjoin a summary, shows the extent of the course of Studies in 1839.

Pupils, one hundred and six—the little juniors not included. Classes examined—four.

Studies—French Grammar, English do.; Arithmetic; Geography; History of England; Roman History; Translation; Rhetoric, French and English; Compositions, prose and verse; Elements of Astronomy; Botany and Mineralogy; Physics and Chemistry, with experiments.

The programme was varied with Vocal and Instrumental Music—the piano, harp and guitar.

On the tables were displayed specimens of writing, drawing and painting; needlework and embroidery.

The third session closed with the Drama, CORIOLANUS—and the DISTRIBUTION OF PRIZES.

Some changes and improvements have naturally been called for, in the course of the past thirty-five years ; the most striking are those which regard the Examination of the pupils. These exercises, as far as regards the solid branches of education, being no longer performed in presence of a public audience, are only the more serious and salutary, as well as more congenial to the taste and feelings both of teachers and pupils. [1]

[1] For Examinations at a recent date see Appendix J.

In closing these rather desultory remarks on the subject of Education in the Convent, we cannot refrain from mentioning again the immense obligations of the Community towards the Bishops of Quebec.

If, in the course of the preceding pages, the paternal solicitude of the chief Pastor of the diocese for all the inmates of the Monastery, has appeared, on every occasion that regarded their welfare, temporal or spiritual ; what shall we say of their judicious and enlightened zeal as exerted to promote the principal object of the Institution, the education of young girls ? that education which is never to lose sight of a double object,—preparing at once, useful members of society, and heirs of the kingdom of heaven.

Although the few extracts we have given from the pastoral exhortations addressed to the Community by our worthy Prelates and Ecclesiastical Superiors, are sufficient to show how much the true interests of the Institution have been forwarded by the Episcopal jurisdiction, yet we would fain enter upon further details.

To the late regretted ARCHBISHOP
BAILLAIRGEON (1853–1870) the Community, individually and collectively, owe
a debt of gratitude, as intimately felt, as
the interest he manifested in their happiness was cordial and effective. With what
evident pleasure he gave his approbation
to the plans for various improvements,
whether as regarded the course of studies,
or the buildings, which the increasing
number of pupils rendered desirable !
During his administration, the dimensions of the Monastery continued to extend. Some of these structures were
approved of the more readily, from
the greater facility they afforded for
placing the Provincial Normal-School for
young girls, within the precincts of the
cloister. This was a project the benevolent Prelate had so much at heart, that
ever after they were admitted (1856)
his Lordship never ceased to testify the
liveliest gratitude towards the Community, as if indebted for a personal favor.[1]

See Appendix K.

At a more recent date, the eminent Prelate who governs the Arch-Diocese of Quebec since 1871, HIS GRACE, THE RT.-REV. E.-A. TASCHEREAU, continuing the traditions of his predecessors, has not ceased to honor the Ursulines with his special protection. The vast proportions which, under his direction, the Monastery has lately assumed, and which will, apparently preclude for long years to come the necessity—we had almost said the possibility—of any further additions to the *Monastery of St. Ursula*, proclaim sufficiently what has been the zeal of our illustrious Prelate for the consolidation of an Institution whose foundations were laid, almost 250 years ago, by our VEN. MOTHER MARIE DE L'INCARNATION.

CHAPTER XXIII.

REMINISCENCES, DUE TO AN INCIDENT OF THE 12TH JULY.

1831.

An animated and novel scene diversified the environs of the Monastery on the 12th of July 1831. The Convent-grounds had been invaded by a company of day-laborers and carpenters, in the midst of whom appeared the architect, with Rev. J. Demers (Sem. of Quebec), and the aged *Père Daulé*, Chaplain of the Ursulines.

Already the roof of the main-building has been scaled ; heavy blows make the shingles fly, the boards and rafters shiver ;—but the centre of interest for all, just now, is the belfry and its cross-surmounted spire. That Cross with its arms pointed by the Fleur-de-lis, remounts to ancient times ; and when, tottering on its base, it is seen descending, many eyes are fixed upon it with affection, as upon a relic of the past. At length, it lies prostrate on the ground; and beside it, the bell that had swung beneath, for the space of one hundred and forty years.

But is not this sheer Vandalism? a wanton make-away-with-old-things, as uncalled for as it is unprecedented? Gentle Reader, do not think we shall readily admit such a supposition. Veneration for all that comes down to us from our " ancient Mothers, " would willingly have preserved that antique belfry, which gave so monastic a look to the Ursuline Convent. But the imperious demand for more room, on account of that interesting population, ever in greater numbers flocking in, had been taken into consideration. A third-story, to be raised upon the foundation-walls built by Ven. Mother Marie de l'Incarnation, was resolved upon ;— in fact, it became a fitting emblem of all the succeeding improvements, which in the space of another half-century would be called for.

Leaving the workmen to continue their labors, let us join the group of Nuns and pupils, who, on that summer evening, when the grounds are again clear of men, surround the piles of fragments, and, testing in playful mood the nearer sound of the bell, question of its past history. Is this the first bell that our Mothers ever had ? Is it the same that used to ring so musically, calling the neophytes to the waters of baptism, or the newly-made Christians to Holy Mass ? Is it that bell which Madame de la Peltrie rang so often, as well as Mother St. Joseph and Sr. St. Laurent ? But, no ;—that favored bell was not long-lived. It melted in that memorable fire of the 31st December, 1650 ; and, according to old records, ungratefully threatened the life of the Ven. Mother Mary of the Incarnation, as she passed, with intrepid step, through the long corridor.

Is it then that other bell which, some years later, swung in the belfry of Madame de la Peltrie's Church, and which tolled so sadly at the two successive funerals of 1672 ?—funerals that made the Nuns feel like orphans, bereaved of a tender mother.

No ;—once more, no ! A second conflagration put an end

"To the swinging and the ringing"

of that bell also : but the Convent rises again from its ruins, and this time, the kind hand of charity furnishes a bell which is destined to out-live its belfry. It was the gift of Madame du Tronchet, a French lady who was ever on the watch to oblige the Ursulines of Quebec. Blessed in grand style some years after its reception, with the Marquis de Beauharnais and the Marchioness de Vaudreuil for its sponsors, the fortunate *Marie-Joseph-Louise-Marguerite* was not demolished when dethroned, in 1830, but placed in due time in the Church-steeple beside another of louder tone. Its clear, yet rather sharp and imperious voice is still heard, alternately with its neighbor's, announcing various hours of the day, from four o'clock in the morning to half-past eight at night.

Now, of steeples also there is a story to be told ; a semi-tragical incident which occurred in 1754, furnishes the occasion.

It was a terrible thunder-storm of that dark December-night. The wind-blowing a perfect hurricane, swept pitiless over the whole country, unroofing houses, overturning barns, and performing other feats, worthy of old Boreas in his worst humor. It shook the Convent tremendously, threatening destruction to every thing less solid than stone walls.

On the following morning, the first sight that greeted the inmates of the cloister, was a church without a steeple ! The wind had borne it off, bell and all, and left it in ruins on the ground. How it cleared the roof without breaking it in, was a question ; but the fact was evident. The cross was a little damaged ; the bell not at all. The same hurricane, which had lasted two hours or more, " had unroofed the barn, and torn the cloister gate from its hinges," causing a devastation which, in all, our Mothers estimated at 2,000 livres.

Of course, another steeple arose in due time; and again the bell was heard calling to prayer: calling at early hours, to awaken the Religious; whether in the golden days of summer, when, at four o'clock, the sky is so glorious that its sight pays the early riser for coming forth from the most refreshing slumbers; whether in winter,

> " In the icy air of night
> While the stars that oversprinkle
> All the heavens, seem to twinkle
> With a crystalline delight :—"

Ever with undeviating punctuality the Bell rings out its solemn peal, calling to prayer, to labor, or to repose : for, within the Monastery, that Bell is the voice of order and authority;—it is the voice of God !

How joyously it rings to usher in the great festivals, as the year goes round ! How cheerful is its tone on that morning, when the little band of white-robed communicants, after long preparations for the Great Day, are admitted for the first time to be Table of the Lord !

How glad, yet solemn is the Bell that announces to the happy novice, that the hour has come for her to pronounce the " good word," her final divorce from the world.

More solemn, yet not of utter sadness, is that other voice of the Convent-Bell, telling that a soul has gone forth from her earthly tenement to meet her Creator.

> " Yet 'tis not weariness of life
> That makes us wish to die ;
> But we are drawn by cords of love,
> From out eternity."

Sometimes we hear it ringing a loud, long and earnest peal, when the cloistered family need not its warning, being already assembled in the choir. Through the air the chime is borne to the whole neighborhood, inviting worshippers to join in spirit, or by their presence, at the sacred function,—the afternoon Benediction Service. " Hasten, it seems to say, hasten ye that are weary and worn with the ungrateful toil of the week. This is the moment when Jesus waits to bless and strengthen you. Come, hasten to adore Him !"

But let us briefly recount the honors, and the end, of that storm-vexed bell, which was precipitated to the ground of a December night, as we have said.

Purchased for our church,—just finished in 1824,—it was in the presence of a goodly company that its blessing or *baptism* took place, the sponsors being the Intendant's son, Mr. Begon, and Miss Elizabeth de Vaudreuil ; the officiating clergymen was Rev. M. de Varennes, V. G.. Twenty years after the accident of the storm, from some unknown cause, the mellow tones of the said bell, suddenly changed to a tinkling and discordant sound, " as unmusical says the Annalist, as an old brass kettle."

It was necessary to provide another ; and our Mothers were willing to have one of larger dimensions. Through some mistake in the order, a bell weighing 850 pounds was sent :—it was heavier than would have been desirable. Blessed

12

with less ceremony than the former, and named *Jean-Olivier*, its reign was inaugurated in 1774.

Having served during a century without any worse accident than an occasional false turn, or a broken bell-rope, let us wish it a continuation of "its clear and musical voice;" although it may still merit the reproach bestowed upon it in its youth, namely, that " it is rather hard to ring."

But another relic of the past has here to be accounted for,—the CROSS, which had towered aloft over the MONASTERY OF ST. URSULA for such a length of years that its origin is lost in obscurity. Would our Readers behold it again? Let them follow —if they may—the long winding alleys of the Nuns' garden, till they reach the highest part of the gradually rising ground. Here, a rocky ledge, grass-grown along its verge, makes a pleasant pathway; while the fractures and angles of the rugged limestone, relieved by mosses and lichens, are enlivened by wild flowers that have outlived the ancient forest. Amid their bloom, stands the old FRENCH CROSS, on a pedestal which is itself a relic, being cut from the trunk of the OLD-ASH-TREE, of historic memory. A rustic arbor, near, would be at home in the midst of this shrubbery,—the elder with its flat corymbs of sweet-scented white-flowers ; the cranberry and red-raspberry bushes, mingling with clusters of golden-rod, buttercups, the star-like white daisy, and fairy-looking campion. The jointed clover and arrow-leaved buckwheat, seem to have a mission here, in trailing over the dark-colored rock. The delicate corydalis and wood-sorrel, the dwarf speedwell, with its pretty blue flowers — miniature forget-me-nots — remind us of solitary glades and untrodden dells amid the hills, far away from city-life.

Oh ! this is the spot to dream of the olden times ! This height, which has preserved through centuries its primitive vegetation, should bear the foot-prints of the little Indian girls, that wandered

here, full of strange, new thoughts of the
Great Spirit, and all his love for them,
after they had listened to the glowing
words of Mother Mary of the Incarnation or Madame de la Peltrie. Here,
perhaps, sat dear Mother St. Joseph, with
a group of little Huron girls, to whom
she was explaining the words of eternal
life ; and here have strayed, at different
hours, all those holy Nuns whose lives
and examples are our greatest encouragement in the pursuit of virtue.

This height, at the present day, is a
favorite haunt, especially in the late afternoon of a summer's Sunday; when the
rays of the declining sun are screened off
by that protecting line of houses along the
street, beyond the cloister-wall. On that
day of rest, the evening recreation brings
out to enjoy the cooling shade, the whole
population of the Monastery. The pupils
have their spacious grounds, bordered
and set out with trees ; their Arcade
built on the plan of the ancient cloisters,
only of lighter materials ;—their croquet —

grounds ; their summer-houses, &c. We, from our station near the old Cross, may hear their merry shouts and calls:—they are to our right, in the environs of *Notre-Dame de-Grace* and *St. Joseph's*, the two modern edifices connected with *St. Augustin's* that constitute the department of the Boarding-school.

Before us, at the distance of some twenty rods, is the building occupied by the Community, *the Holy-Family*, built in 1686 ; its two modern wings, *St. Thomas* and *Marie-de-l'Incarnation*, giving it an aspect, massive, and almost severe. Beyond, at the distance of twenty rods more, is a mod·ern structure — the Externs—replacing *Madame de la Peltrie's house* ; while, adjoining the *Church*, *St. Ursula* and *St. Angela*, along the street, connect the cloister, on that side, with the outer-world. [1]

This garden-field, set with fruit-trees and flowering shrubs, the plum, cherry

---

[1] See Appendix, L. for the dimensions of these various buildings, indicated by Italics.

and apple, the lilac, the mock-orange,
&c., stretches away to the north and the
west of our rustic seat, in many a shady
walk. It is the resort of more than
twenty species of birds ; warblers of various song, sparrows, finches, the social
robin, the hungry chatterer, the lively
swallow ; and weary voyager-birds, of
many a name, seek this quiet spot for a
few days' rest and refreshment. These
denizens of the woods make melody
here ; but the noise of the Town reaches
us no more than if we were still surrounded by the wild scenery, that formed
the landscape two hundred and forty
years ago.

It is a welcome solitude in the midst of
a City;—a place for study—for musing, —
for repose; and even—when we raise our
eyes to that CROSS—for prayer:—

O CRUX AVE, SPES UNICA !

CHAPTER XXIV.

THE MONASTERY NARROWLY ESCAPES A TOTAL CONFLAGRATION.

1834.

Every time the 12th of January has come round since 1834, the Nuns, after Mass, are heard joining in the hymn of thanksgiving : " *Praise ye the Lord all ye nations ; praise him all ye people !* LAUDA-TE DOMINUM, OMNES GENTES." In the course of the day, some of the pupils, or the younger members of the Novitiate, are apt to inquire : Why was the *Laudate* said this morning—and the story of the Fire is rehearsed.—The most minute de-tails never seem superfluous ; so imminent was the danger, and so providential the escape from a total conflagration.

First, it is explained, that an out-house, or shed, some twenty feet long, stood adjacent to the kitchen, on the southwest of

the main building *St. Augustin's*, serving
as a store-room for fuel, and a cold pantry.

A lighted candle—it is supposed —had
been unwarily left there, late in the evening, upon a shelf; and in burning down
to the socket, it set fire to the combustible
matter near.

This fire had been creeping from one
smouldering mass to another for several
hours, when it was discovered, at two
o'clock in the morning, by the crackling
sound of the earthen-ware it had reached
in the kitchen.

The Infirmarian, thus awakened from
her sleep, had only to step into the corridor
to behold the flames issuing from an aper-
ture in the door of the apartment beneath.
Without losing her presence of mind, she
ran to awaken the sick; and then to warn
the Nuns in their dormitory, and the
boarders who were sleeping in the adjacent
building.

While this was being done, and all were
dressing in haste, the Convent bell had
sounded the alarm; and the fire, seizing the

roof of the shed where it had originated, was perceived in various directions. The Convent steward and the domestics, were hurrying in. Our nearest neighbours, Judge Vaufelson and his son, Hon. Thos. Aylwin, and R. E. Caron, Esq., (later Lieut.-Governor) met, in the conventual porch, the Chaplain, Rev. C. Gauvreau, and at his request undertook to guard the front door, in order to prevent a promiscuous entrance ; for the terrible tocsin was ringing, and awakening all the City. Col. McDougall had called out his troops, and the Convent grounds, although piled with snow, were filling with crowds of citizens of every class, all anxious to render service. The Seminary priests, Rev. J. Demers, Rev. L. Gingras, Rev. John Holmes, and their colleagues, constituted themselves the special guardians of the Monastery ; their day students, rivalling with the regular firemen, were so prompt that their engine was the first brought into action.

In the mean time the pupils had quietly followed their mistresses to the chapel,

to implore the protection of Heaven, and
thence to the Extern-school-house, where
they would be in safety from any imme-
diate danger. The Nuns, as they passed
with hurried step, dropped on their knees
before the Tabernacle for a moment's
prayer, and preserved their calmness,
while hastening to save every thing that
could be removed from the apartments
nearest the danger.

The night was every moment becoming more illuminated by the spreading
flames. Now, the guarded conventual
door opens to admit the Governor's
Aid de Camp, who must see the Mother
Superior immediately. Rev. Mother St.
Henry, calm and self-possessed in the
midst of the confusion, promptly appears,
and the messenger delivers to her an
open letter. It was a pressing invitation
on the part of Lord and Lady Aylmer for
the Nuns to accept an asylum in the
Castle ;— the apartments were already
being warmed and put in readiness, and
carriages were in waiting at the Convent
door.

But all hope was not yet lost; and on every side the most vigorous efforts were directed to arrest the progress of the conflagration. A file of soldiers through the long corridors, connected the kitchen with the cistern in the interior courtyard, and buckets of water passed rapidly from hand to hand. The garden-cistern, buried in snow-drifts, was uncovered to supply the fire-engines, working on the outside.

Yet there came a moment, when it seemed that the destructive element was doomed to have the mastery.

The cellar beneath the kitchen, into which the floor had fallen, was one burning mass of coals; the Infirmary above it, the attic, and the roof, were on fire. The refectory beyond the kitchen, where the pine wainscoting and ceiling, were as dry as one hundred and fifty years could make them, was so filled with smoke that one who penetrated to explore it [Judge E. Bedard] only succeeded in making his exit by creeping on his hands and knees:

he had ascertained that the beams and
ceiling were burning ! While the least
delay must prove fatal, shouts from the
firemen announced that the pumps were
freezing, and could not be worked without larger supplies of hot water. At this
crisis—one to make the strongest heart
quail in view of the impending calamity—
the loud cry of faith went up to Heaven ;—
Masses were promised ; the pupils were
called into the chapel, where many of
the nuns had fled to pray ; all our holy
Protectors were called upon to interpose.

One of the nuns had confided the relic,
called "*Ribbon of St. Amabilis*" to the hands
of the Chaplain, as worthier than her
own to obtain a miracle ; and he had fast-
ened the precious badge on the door of
the refectory, with a fervent prayer for
the preservation of the Convent. Another
friend of the Ursulines, transported by
compassion and the extremity of the
peril, rushes into the Infirmary, and there,
prostrate on the floor, beneath which
the flames are raging, he prays like

Moses on the Mount, with outstretched arms, invoking the Divine clemency upon the sacred mansion, every stone of which, telling of past favors, pleads for their continuance. [1]

That mingled concert of sighs, and vows, and prayers, was heard !

Of a sudden, new energy seemed infused into every heart and every arm. From one point to another, the wild flames were driven, or kept in check, till, at length, the most violent of the elements was under control. At seven o'clock, most of the engines had ceased to work. People could approach and look upon the charred remains of the small wooden building which had put the whole establishment in such jeopardy ; they could behold the denuded kitchen, with blackened and crevassed walls ; the yawning cellar where smoked the winter's provisions ; the refectory, with its ceiling broken in, through half its length,

---

[1] This friend was the Rev. John Holmes.

and a pine beam that should have burnt like tinder, only marked by a few inches of charcoal : the Infirmary, without windows, and the roof above the attic, partly consumed.

It was Sunday,—and at 8 o'clock, the Convent bell rang again its signal for Mass. Oh ! with what grateful hearts did the Nuns and their dear pupils, kneel around that altar, to join the Eucharistic Sacrifice,—that adequate thanksgiving for all blessings, whether spiritual or temporal.

The Convent grounds were still occupied by the troops, in case the fire should again re-appear; but when another hour's tranquillity had proved that all danger had ceased, Col. McDougall,—who had declared that he was ready to lose his life, if necessary in order to save the Convent, — gave the word of command, and with a light heart, led off his faithful auxiliaries.

The Extern Seminary students would not lose so good an opportunity to manifest their chivalry. Their pump, which had won the prize for being the first to render service, remained all day on the grounds, with a guard around it, to give assistance, in case of need. They probably deemed it a fortunate occurrence for them, that the fire rekindled in the cellar, giving them an opportunity of proving their good will by working to extinguish it. During that Sunday and the following days, visits of congratulation and sympathy succeeded each other, till it seemed as if all the ladies of Quebec, from Lady Aylmer to good dame Jalbert, wife of our steward, had been to the Convent : they must compliment the pupils on their quiet, orderly behaviour; they must assure themselves that none of the Nuns have been seriously incommoded ; they must see the ruins, and only after being on the spot, could they fully realiz· how imminent had been the danger.

Yet, not even the Nuns, perhaps,fully appreciated the protection of Heaven over the Monastery,until, only a fortnight later, the old Castle of St. Louis, which had withstood three sieges, took fire at mid-day, and in spite of all the efforts of the troops and the aid of a dozen of fire-engines, was entirely consumed.

No ! it was not in vain that so many vows had been offered for the preservation of the Monastery. Bishop Signay acquitted his promise, on the following morning, by singing High Mass at the Cathedral, which became a public act of thanksgiving by the crowds who attended. On Tuesday, another High Mass was sung in the Convent Chapel, in the midst of a large concourse. Clergymen showed their sympathy by saying their Mass at the altar, where so many prayers had been offered in the moment of danger; and thus through the octave, was manifested a spirit of faith and a charity, which we love to find the same as in the olden times.

The accident had only resulted in a loss, comparatively insignificant ; yet, for the moment, it was an embarrassing situation, in a family of about one hundred and forty persons, to have at hand, neither cooking utensils, table service, nor food. By the delicate attention of friends, and their unbounded kindness, all these. wants were supplied with the utmost liberality. At the dinner hour, the table, both for the nuns and the pupils, was spread with profusion. Now it was Lady Aylmer, sending from the Castle, roasted surloins and choice viands, the Governor adding his dozen of wines ; so that our Nuns feared to resemble the rich man who fared sumptuously every day. Now it was the Nuns of the Hotel-Dieu, with a full measure of wholesome soup and steaming vegetables. All the more wealthy ladies in Upper Town, had their turn in furnishing a repast for the inmates of the cloister, before a new state of things could be organized. Benefactions came in various forms; plates and dishes for the Nuns' table ; cooking utensils, coarse linen for kitchen use : provisions ; money :—all is duly entered, with the donors' names, and many an expression of gratitude, on the pages of the Annals.

The *Quebec Gazette*[1], rendering an account of the fire, has the following remarks :—

"In a Convent of Religious ladies, leading a retired and pious life, such an accident as threatened the Ursulines, must have appeared very distressing. Yet these ladies displayed courage, activity, and self-possession, in the highest degree. The Governor-General had hastened to offer them the Castle, in case they should be obliged to abandon their house : happily, their own intelligent efforts, aided by the zeal and energy of their friends, prevented the painful necessity of accepting the alternative."

Then, follows from the Nuns, a Card of Thanks, "most grateful and sincere, to His Excellency and Staff, to the Officers and froops, to the gentlemen of the City Council, the Magistrates, the Seminary Priests and Students, to the Fire-Company, as well as to the numerous citizens of

---

[1] Edited by John Neilson, Esq.

every class for their timely and efficient aid. The Religious were most sensible to the reserve and politeness, manifested by all towards the inmates of the cloister.

"They acknowledge with gratitude the services of the watch kept around their goods, as well as around the ruins, and which was continued till Monday morning, in case the fire might break out anew."

The Annalist has not forgotten to commend the good conduct of the pupils, their docility and the cheerfulness with which they accepted all the inconveniences entailed by the accident.

. This most providential escape from one of the greatest of temporal misfortunes, calls to mind another, of more recent date, the particulars of which will long be remembered in the Convent.

It has been recorded in a little poetical effusion, which we shall venture to place before our readers, not for any merit it could claim as a poem, but for its motive and occasion.

THE MEMORABLE TWENTIETH MAY!
1804.

(A tribute of gratitude to our venerated Chaplain, Rev.
George L. LEMOINE, who, on the occasion commemorated
in the following lines. periled his life to save the church
from being destroyed by fire.)

It was the evening hour,—a cloudless sky :
The moon had wheel'd her silver orb on high
With one attendant star :—the others, veiled,
Stood at a distance; or, on ether paled.
The city's din had ceased,—no sound of care,
For Night was stilling, with her dreamy air,
Earth's joys and sorrows; hushing all to rest :
E'en as a mother, clasping to her breast
Her wearied infant, lulls it to repose.—
Around the Convent, too, the shadows close ;
Light heart are slumbering at this early hour;
Of youth and innocence sleep is the dower.

————But whence that sudden glare, as noon-day
Is't some volcano bursting on the night ?   [bright ?
Hark ! now the tocsin sounds—the city wakes
To view the wreathing flames, tossing on high,
And casting wide a storm of angry flakes,
That fall, like meteors, on the mansions nigh—
Built as of tinder.—See ! the flames are driven
Like fierce tornado.—Onward still they come,
And now—but, oh ! forbid it, gracious Heaven !—
They reel, they dash around our cloistered Home :
All, all is threatened ! Help ! ye Angels strong !
Heavenly Protectors, who have watched us long.—

Mary, dear Mother! oh! protect thy shrine;
Say, shall it perish?—Perish,—when 'tis thine?
Hark! from the streets, the cry that rends the air;
"Save, save the chapel! Firemen, onward! there—
Right thro' that narrow street, direct your aim."
But, firemen—can they rush into the flame?
'Tis on them, like a sea, whose waves devour!
On, on it rolls! Oh! unpropitious hour!
Who then shall do the deed, with danger rife—
To save the Convent, who peril his life?

——Ah! *one* was there! a generous, daring Friend—
Into the furnace flames that round him spend
Their rage, he rushes! nerv'd with purpose high,
To save that sacred fane, or with it die!
There waged he conflict dire—yet, hap'ly, brief,—
For firemen now have come to his relief.
And citizens are there, all friends most true,—
A venerable prelate, clergy, too!— — — —
A shout goes up—"That church must not burn
And hundreds join *him*, battling there alone. [down;"
"Haste to the rescue!" Some the chapel-wall
Ascend with ladders, till their axes fall
Upon the cindered roof—others, within,
Bear succor where most needed,—while the din
Of crashing timbers, hissing flames, and cries
Of eager cheering, from that crowd arise;
Still fierce the rival elements contend,
And for the mastery their rage expend.

. . . .

But where are they, and say in what affright,
The inmates of the cloister on this night ?
Would ye behold them ?—Calmness still is theirs ;
They're aiding, too,—oh ! with what ardent prayers !
Before the altar, see them prostrate now—
The Mother speaks for all the solemn vow :—
" Protect thine own, O Lord !—in Joseph's name
We come, Thy ever gracious aid to claim !"
And swift from anxious hearts went up the prayer
That Heaven accepts—the prayer of thousands there—
For see : the flames retire !—It is the breath
Of Him who, in that night-wind's veering, saith
Unto that sea of fire : " Here be thou stayed,
Enough the ruin thy red waves have made."
——Now from the crowd went up the joyous cry :
" The danger's o'er !—Virgins ye need not fly
Your cloistered Home !"— — — — — —
— — — — —They look, and with amaze ;—
" The danger's o'er !—To God be all the praise !"

Ursuline Convent, Quebec.

May 1864. [1]

---

[1] The fire on this occasion destroyed two dwelling-houses
(with sheds adjoining), forming the angle of Donnacona
and Parlor streets, opposite the church of the Ursulines.

CHAPTER XXV.

THE BI-CENTENNIAL.

1839.

ιe preceding pages have displayed
re our readers, something of the Mon-
·y's past; they have seen the protect-
Hand of Providence ever extended
it, as two centuries have rolled on,
ι August first, 1639 to the same date,
).

o doubt such an anniversary was one
ǝ celebrated in the Convent with gra-
le and pious rejoicings. The spiritual
·vation, to which it manifestly invited,
foreseen from the beginning of the
·. The examples of the venerated
Foundresses were made a special
y, and the words of the Apostle "*Be*
·newed in Spirit," seemed to have their
ication to every individual soul. But

the preparations carried on, in this interior world of the spirit, being intended for the eye of God alone, are mostly invisible to mortal sight, and scarcely come within the scope of ordinary description.

Exterior preparations were not neglected. The Chapel, which, in 1739, shone forth in its new painting and gilding, needed some repair, and the decorations were to be as elaborate as possible. Our cloistered artists, vying with each other in their efforts to honor the occasion, put into requisition the pencil and easel, and every hour of leisure saw the results of ingenuity and good will. Emblematical and commemorative paintings, on transparent tissues, filled the windows; banners, skilfully wrought, and light banderoles, inscribed with appropriate mottoes, streamed, at various heights, around the sanctuary, alternating with festoons of evergreen and wreaths of bloom. The altar presented one bright array of lights and flowers. Enthusiasm, moderated by religious feeling, and that solemnity attached to things we shall never see again, prevailed throughout the Community, and reached its climax on the great day.

The large number of Masses celebrated at the three altars; the skilful execution of one of Mozart's Masses by the Nuns and the pupils, while at the grand altar officiated the Bishop of Quebec, and sixty Clergymen filled the sanctuary; the singing of Vespers by the same dignified assembly on the one hand, and the Nuns from their choir on the other; the remarkably appropriate oration, by Rev. C. F. Baillairgeon (then Pastor, afterwards Archbishop, of Quebec;) the Benediction of the Blessed Sacrament; the *Te Deum* chanted to the fullest swell of the new organ; these were the principal features of the DAY. They were sufficient to mark the commemoration as one of the most thrilling interest:—a day never to be recalled to mind without emotion by any who took part in its festivities. As at the first Centennial, the *Communion of Saints* was not forgotten : the dear deceased had their part in the festival, and thirty

13

Masses were offered for their more speedy admission to the realms of bliss.

The only circumstance that reminded one with sadness of the changes that TWO HUNDRED YEARS may bring, was the absence of the Indian race from the celebration.

Was it not especially for them that in 1639, the Ursulines and the *Hospitalières* had landed on the beach of a wild and savage country ? The poor aborigenes had been among the first to reap the fruits of such heroic charity:—but to day there exist only scattered remnants of their race, destined to a gradual extinction. Surely no one can reflect upon such a fate without commiseration, nor stand unmoved beside the grave of a people. In the few rude hamlets that still remain to them in Lower Canada, the tradition of what the Ursulines have done for them has been preserved, and will only perish with the last of their race.

If we regard the political aspect of Canada in 1839, in contrast to its early

times, we remark that for many a year
no shadow of war had overcast its pros-
pects with gloom. There had been indeed
some recent disturbances; but they were
not wide-spread nor lasting. There were
painful memories in the city of Quebec,
of the terrible visitations of 1832 and
1834, [1] which could not be forgotten.
Yet Canada was to experience again
"that she is a country guarded in a
special manner by Divine Providence :—
that at the moment when all would seem
lost there would arise unforeseen succor
and events favorable to its prosperity."

Thus from one advantage to another,
its chart of history shows, at last, in 1867
the advent of its Independence, meekly
granted under the name of " Dominion ; [2]"
its three million of inhabitants, enjoying
civil and religious liberty, with rights

[1] The Asiatic cholera in 1832, made in Quebec
3,451 victims : in 1834, 2509. It appeared a third
time in 1849, and again in 1851–52, and 1854, but
its three last apparitions were far less fatal.

[2] See Appendix M.

and privileges sufficient to make every citizen secure and happy, as far as human institutions can make him so.

But let us return to the cloister, and to our date of August 1st. 1839.

To the Nuns the contrast of that present with the past, was of a nature to excite their devout gratitude. In the calamity just alluded to, that had darkened the land [1832 and 1834], filling Quebec especially, with mourning on every side, the Convent had stood unharmed, [1] proving once more the salubrity of the site, chosen for the home of the Ursulines by their incomparable Foundress ; and manifesting the kind protection of Heaven over an Institution devoted to the most beneficent of works, the instruction of youth.

Within a few years, also, the same kind Providence had brought them a signal protector, "a second Founder" in the

---

[1] There were two cases of the dreaded malady but neither proved fatal.

person of their venerated chaplain, Rev. Thomas Maguire, Vicar General of the Diocese of Quebec; to whose merits the Bishops of Canada had lately rendered a striking homage, by twice deputing him on a voyage to Europe, on business of importance to all the country.

To him the Ursulines with their ecclesiastic Superior, had confided the temporal affairs of the Monastery : and to his intelligent investigations, his patient and laborious research, his foresight and firmness, his experience, his spirit of order and economy, they are happy to ascribe the prosperity which has replaced a labyrinth of pecuniary difficulties. These preoccupations of a temporal nature, however, had never interfered with the higher consideration of maintaining the practice of religious perfection, the spirit of regularity and mortification, of which the life of our excellent Friend was so encouraging a model. From 1835 to 1854, the Community witnessed the indefatigable labors of their devoted Chaplain,

with a deep sense of their own ever increasing obligations. At this last mentioned date, just as the fine new Boarding-
school (*Notre-Dame-de-Grace*,) with its spacious halls, its new system of heat and
ventilation, its accommodations of every
kind, was ready for use, the venerable
hand which had subscribed with joy, to
the plan of this delightful residence for
the pupils of the Ursulines, the heart that
had blessed the project and rejoiced in
its execution, were cold in death. At the
age of eighty years, of which fifty-five had
been devoted to the arduous duties of the
priesthood, our beloved Father, the never-
to-be-forgotten Friend of the Ursulines
and their pupils, passed to his reward in
the bosom of God, whom he had faith-
fully and fervently served from his earliest youth.

After this tribute, however feeble, to
the memory of our worthy friend, REV.
THOMAS MAGUIRE, and the mention of so
recent a date as 1854, how can we refrain from signalizing the continuation of
the favors of Heaven in the appointment

of a successor, equally qualified for the important charge ? When, at a later period, contemporary events shall have become the domain of history, grateful will be the task to recount the inappreciable services rendered the Community by our present excellent Chaplain, REV. G. L. LEMOINE :—whether in the spiritual direction of souls, and in the department of the Instruction of youth ; whether in the providential movement that has brought into closer union the widely disseminated family of St. Ursula, and given new life to the devotion to St. Angela, that precious means of keeping alive the *Sacred-fire*, the primitive spirit of her Institution ; whether as the zealous advocate and special promoter of an enterprize, as laborious as it is dear, not only to the heart of the Ursulines of Quebec and of the whole Order, but to all Canada, an enterprise the happy termination of which we may now safely predict : namely, the Canonization of our Foundress, VEN. MOTHER MARY OF THE INCARNATION,

Another duty not less congenial, remains to us in these last pages of the *Glimpses of the Monastery*. It is to offer a tribute of grateful affection, to the revered and honored names of Rev. Mother Adelaide Plante of St. Gabriel, and Rev. Mother Isabelle McDonald of St. Andrew.

The long period of thirty-six years (1836–1872) assigned by Divine Providence, in the choice of the Community, to these two remarkable Superiors, justifies us in presenting them to our readers, although contemporary history is not to be expected here.

In 1839, Rev. Mother St. Gabriel had just been re-elected for a second term. In 1842, Rev. Mother St. Andrew took her place at the helm; and thus alternately, till the latter had governed twelve years, and the former, twenty-four.

Of different national origin, and in many respects of different characters, their mutual esteem and trust, their union of heart and unity of sentiment could not have been more complete, had they been sisters by birth.

To the more deeply meditative cast of Mother St Andrew's mind, difficulties must have ever appeared in their full dimensions : yet her generosity, her love of duty, would enable her to surmount them with intrepidity.

Rev. Mother St. Gabriel bore with a light heart the burden of the Superiority, as little moved by its solicitudes as by its honors. Equally zealous and conscientious, the decisions of both were sure; and, in counsel, their gifts were of the highest order. Neither ever undertook any thing of importance without consulting the other, and each placed, without hesitation, her chief confidence in the other's judgment. Deep sensibilities, a heart quickly touched by another's weal or woe, distinguished Mother St. Andrew : a world-wide charity, a great noble soul, without a shadow or blemish, was not less the characteristic of Mother St. Gabriel.

All that regarded the duties of the
religious state ; the observance of the
rule, the religious vows, the advancement of each soul in perfection ; all that
related to charity or the preservation of
the primitive spirit of the House, was in-
finitely precious in the eyes of both these
worthy Superiors.

Eminently conservative, at the same
time that they knew how to appreciate
whatever was really advantageous in
modern inventions or appliances, there
was never any unnecessary delay in introducing improvements, especially into
the department of the pupils. They knew
how to draw the line between the useful and the superfluous, the convenient
and the purely ornamental.   •

Following the footsteps of the admirable Mother St. Henry, their predecessor,
they patronized and encouraged the new
studies introduced, as well as the talents
of the Sisters employed in teaching.

The Museum of Natural History increased its catalogue, especially in Orni-

thology and Entomology ; a full Apparatus, suitable for young ladies, was provided for Chemistry and Physics ; valu-
able additions were made to the Libraries,
&c., &c.

There are other particulars to be mentioned here, in which pupils of the present
day, will find a special interest. When
dispersing so joyfully in July for your
summer Vacations, forget not, dear Young
Ladies, that this pleasant annual inter-
ruption in your studies commenced in
1843, under the superiority of Rev.
Mother St. Andrew. The substitute for
a regular Vacation, had been, in previous times, the grant of a monthly holiday, which the pupils had permission
to spend in the bosom of their families,
or if strangers, at the houses of their
friends.

Many benevolent ladies of Quebec, remembered on the holiday that some were
utter strangers to the City, and inviting
them together to their houses, entertained

them with an affability and kindness never to be forgotten[1].

The Annual Retreat for ex-pupils commenced under the superintendence of the
worthy Mother St. Gabriel in August,
1862.

Four years later, the summons of death
was suddenly heard—suddenly for the
Community, but not for venerable Mother
St. Andrew, who in her 70th year,
just re-elected Superior, laid down the
burden of life, as cheerfully as she
would have relinquished her charge.
The dawn of an eternal day was at hand ;
nor could the Angel of death efface the
smile from those dear lips that became
cold while breathing a last prayer.........

If, in that better life, the happy soul has
still an interest in any of the concerns of
this world, Mother St. Andrew must surely rejoice with us, when the period of
the Annual Retreat brings a hundred or
more of the ex-pupils to follow these salu-

[1] Such in 1833–1840 were the hon. families For-
syth, Fraser, Massue, Langevin, Painchaud.

tary Exercises...Worldliness cannot have
enveloped the heart very deeply, when
there is such joy, on their part, in breathing once more the atmosphere of peace
that pervades the cloister ; when, with the
simplicity of children, these young ladies
cheerfully offer themselves to be guided
anew by their Convent-Mothers in the
ways of piety and wisdom.

As to REV. MOTHER ST. GABRIEL, placed still at the head of the Community
by her rank of profession, her four-score
years, and by the unbounded affection
that surrounds her, it should not be con-
sidered an indiscretion if her name were
inscribed here in golden letters. In celebrating her second Golden Jubilee,—the
60th anniversary of her consecration to
God, July 20th, 1875, the Community-
Hall offered a spectacle worthy of our
ancient traditions. It was a festival in
which piety, poetry, music and mirth,
entwined their offerings with affection
and gratitude. It was a goodly sight to
behold that venerable and beloved Moth-

er, crowned with her bridal-wreath of
white roses, seated on her modest throne;
having on her right and left, five other
aged Mothers who had passed through
the honors of a Jubilee; receiving the con-
gratulations of that long file of sixty professed choir Nuns, followed by the twenty
lay-Sisters and fifteen white-veiled Novices.
If such a celebration, foreshadowing the
sunset of life, bears with it a tinge of sadness, it is of the nature of that which we
may feel at the evening hour, when the
sky is gorgeous with those bright colors
which foretell a still more glorious coming day. What greater pledge of a happy
reunion in HEAVEN can there be, than to
live in PEACE, UNION and CHARITY here
below !

SUPERIORS FROM 1739 TO 1872.

[*List continued from page 202, Vol. II.*]

11. [eleventh Sup.] Rev. Mother Marie-Anne Migeon of the Nativity :—

Sup. from 1735 to 1741 :—1744 to 1750 : —1753–
1760=19 years.

12. Rev. Mother Geneviève La Grange of St. Louis :
—1741 to 1744=3 years.

13. Rev. Mother Geneviève Boucher of St. Pierre :
—1750 to 1753=3 years.

14. Rev. Mother Esther Wheelwright of the Infant
Jesus :—1760 to 1766 :—1769 to 1772=9 years.

15. Rev. Mother Marguerite Davanne of St. Louis
de Gonzague :—1766 to 1769 :—1772 to 1778 :—
1781 to 1787=15 years.

16. Rev. Mother Antoinette Poulin of St. Francis :
—1778 to 1781=3 years.

17. Rev. Mother Marie-Charlotte Brassard of St.
Clare :—1787 to 1793=6 years.

18. Rev. Mother Marie-Anne-Louise Taschereau of
St. Fr. Xavier :—1793 to 1799 :—1805 to 1811 :
—1815 to 1818=15 years.

19. Rev. Mother Marguerite Marchand of St. Ursula :
—1799 to 1805 :—1811 to 1815, (dec.)=10 years.

20. Rev. Mother Mary-Louisa McLoughlin of St.
Henry :—1818 to 1824:—1830 to 1836=12 years.

21. Rev. Mother Julie Berthelot of St. Joseph :—
1824 to 1827=3 years.

22. Rev. Mother Margaret Boissonnault of St. Monica :—1827 to 1830=3 years.

23. Rev. Mother Adelaïde Plante of St. Gabriel :—
1836 to 1842 :—1848 to 1854 :—1857 to 1863 :—
1866 to 1872 :—24 years.

24. Rev. Mother Isabella McDonald of St. Andrew :
—1842 to 1848 :—1854 to 1857 :—1863 to 1866 :
=12 years (dec. in Office).

CHAPTER XXVI.

PATRONS AND PATRONESSES:

When a youthful candidate for the Religious life has been admitted to the society of the cloister, one of the first ascetical books presented to her study, is the " Directory of Novices," the Guide-Book in the new world to which she is being introduced. She peruses its pages with mingled curiosity and admiration ; but nowhere, perhaps, does she feel more impressed with the angelic life that is set before her, than in the chapter that treats of her duties towards the inhabitants of heaven, the Saints.

" The Religious soul, says her Guide, having abandoned the world and forgotten, according to the advice of the Psalmist, 'her people and her father's house,' enters into a strange land, contracts new alliances, and becomes as the Apostle says, 'a fellow-citizen with the Saints.'

"This should animate her with respect, confidence, and devotion, towards all the inhabitants of the Heavenly Jerusalem," with whom she has henceforth the privilege to be associated.

The Blessed Virgin is to be honored as her " first and principal Superior ;" St. Joseph, as the special Patron and protector of the Monastery of Quebec :—but other patrons of the Order there are, with whom she must form acquaintance :— St. Augustin, St. Ursula and St. Angela. She must imitate their virtues and have recourse, in filial confidence, to their intercession.

" Thus, continues her Guide, making the Saints thy companions, thou shalt attain sanctity ; and having thy conversation more in heaven than upon the earth, thou shalt become thyself celestial."

Encouraged by these magnificent promises, she resolves to study the lives and meditate the examples of her holy patrons.

She has not failed to hear already of St. Augustin, one of the brightest geniuses of the early ages of the Church. The Rule he composed for the Monasteries of his time—the fourth century—and which is still followed by many Religious Orders, has formed as many saints, perhaps, as it contains letters.

But St. Ursula and St. Angela may be less known—to our Readers, as well as to her ;—therefore we may be allowed the pleasure of introducing them, by a few brief remarks.

Wonderful legends, tracing back to the fifth century, surround the name of ST. URSULA ; legends illustrated by painting and sculpture, and celebrated by monuments as enduring as they are majestic and venerable. The historic Church of St. Ursula and her thousands of companions, stands at a short distance from the beautiful Cathedral of Cologne : the Field of the Martyrs is not far away ; and

the Golden Chamber piled high with
many a gilded casket, enclosing their
relics, is open to the devout, or the inqui-
sitive traveller.

As to the stupendous events handed
down to us by the legend, some may
adopt that version which gives to the
Princess Ursula the Isle of Albion as her
home, and the land of Brittany as the
term of her voyage ; the assembling of so
many young girls around her, is then explained as the result of a compact between the Prince of Cornwall, her father,
and the late Conqueror of Gaul :—others
may prefer that more marvellous and fascinating narrative, which tells of stranger
vicissitudes; of long negotiations, of celestial visions, by which the future Martyr
is warned to prepare by a long pilgrimage
for the glorious but sanguinary fate that
awaits her :—on either hand we have the
same catastrophe—the arrival of the voyagers on the borders of the Rhine at Cologne ; the presence of the barbarous
cohorts of the Huns; and, finally, the
martyrdom of the virginal troop by those

vindictive and ferocious warriors, disappointed of their prey.

Leaving the field of conjecture and dis-
cussion, we find St. Ursula honored as the
Patroness of learning and piety, long before the Religious Order, bearing her
name, arose in the Church. Cologne itself was the centre of a great Confrater-
nity in honor of the Virgin Martyr, under
the title of The Bark of St. Ursula.

The renowned University of Sorbona
(1200 A. D.), was placed under the patronage of the same great Princess, whose
wise ,precepts and fervent exhortations
had guided her youthful charge so effect-
ually, that in the direst extremity of peril,
they all remained faithful to their duty,
and to their God.

The prerogative ascribed to St. Ursula,
making her the Patroness of Institutions
of learning, renders it easy to account for
the choice St. Angela made of her name
in founding an Order exclusively devoted
- to the pious education of female youth.
The humble Foundress, at the same time,

had found the means to avoid leaving her own name to her followers, who will not be known as ANGELINES but as URSULINES.

The new Institution of ST. ANGELA—the first of the kind, known in the Church, —dates from the year 1535 ; its cradle was the ancient city of Brescia in the north of Italy.

The Foundress was born in the little town of Dezanzano, on Lake Garda, six leagues from Brescia, of parents rich in piety and virtue, more than in the wealth that perishes with its possessor. In those precious years when the future lot of children is shadowed forth by the formation of their character, Angela was edified by the bright examples of a truly Christian household : her faith was strengthened, and she began from that tender age to walk in the ways of wisdom and sanctity.

Trials came early to wean this soul from every earthly attachment. An orphan, and bereaved of an only sister, she was not abandoned : kind relatives continued to protect her childhood, till its promise of excellence ripened into the practice of every virtue.

Passing unnoted the various incidents of a life, mostly serene, and at all times pure and blameless, we hasten to remark the circumstances that accompanied the founding of the new Order.

It was in a vision, that Angela, like the prophets of old, first learned what great things God demanded of her. A mysterious ladder, reaching from earth to heaven, was displayed before her; troops of virgins appeared mounting the steep ascent, each one being attended and aided by a bright-winged Angel. The words, " Angela thou shalt live to found an Order of Virgins in the Church, of which this spectacle is the figure," struck her wondering ear—and the celestial vision disappeared.

The enterprise seemed so far above her strength, that Angela hesitated long, and waited for further intimations of the

Divine Will : she only undertook its execution after repeated consultations with her ecclesiastical Superiors, and when, by a new communication from Heaven, she had learned that further delay would not be acceptable to God.

Already the companions of the Saintly Maiden, were her associates in good works;—visiting the sick, succoring the poor, comforting the distressed. To these practices, Angela now joined the instruction of youth; and gradually there assembled around her a company, filled with the noblest zeal for their own perfection and the salvation of souls. The new Congregation received its first rules and its double spirit from the venerable Foundress:—it was a legacy of inestimable price. Alas ! the earthly career of the Virgin of Brescia was drawing to a close. Having given the first impulse to the Order, she seemed, like holy Simeon of old, to have lived enough. But even during the few years that she was spared to direct her spiritual daughters, their number had increased to sixty. Like Moses, on the

borders of the Promised Land, she foresaw the wonderful multiplication of her
Institution and the blessings that were destined to crown her labors. With calmness
she bade adieu to her beloved daughters
in Christ, plainly foretelling the stability
of the Order which she declared would
endure to the end of time.

It is not within the brief limits assigned
us here that we can trace the truly
wonderful extension of the Order, first
through Italy, then to France and to the
other countries of Europe, till, at the
close of the 18th century, the Revolutionary Tornado found over three hundred
Houses to destroy, in the kingdom of
France alone.

The opportuneness of the Institution
of the Ursulines, has been often remarked. It was at an epoch when the perils
of new doctrines, the scandal of great
and public defections, rendered more
necessary than ever the solid instruction
of youth in the tenets of the true Church.
The heart of woman, especially to whose

guidance the souls of men, during the plastic season of childhood, are confided, needs to be a fount of wisdom and piety. It can only become that "spring of living water," fit to profit others to eternal life, by being itself saturated with the dews of heaven.

It remains to us to state the extent of the Order of St. Ursula at the present day. A list of the principal Monasteries in France, where they had been swept away just before the commencement of the nineteenth century, shows that the arduous task of restoration has been crowned with a success truly providential. One hundred and fifty Convents, inheriting the spirit of St. Angela like their predecessors, continue the pious labor of the instruction of young girls ;— some of them on the very sites whence the ancient Ursulines were driven into exile, or conducted to martyrdom.[1]

[1] Twenty-five Ursulines, in France, had the supreme honor and happiness of sealing with their blood their fidelity to their duty and their religion. The others were not pursued to such an extremity.

14

In America, including the two Spanish Communities of the Island of Cuba, there are twenty-two Convents of Ursulines. In Ireland there are four ; in Belgium thirty-two ; in Italy, Holland, Austria, Germany and the rest of Europe, others, to the number total of about three hundred. These Convents assemble, it is calculated, as many as twelve thousand Religious, who impart the benefits of a pious and solid education to at least one hundred thousand young girls.

If, in conclusion, we might express the most ardent wish of our heart, it would be that the words uttered by a venerable member of the Catholic hierarchy, might ever and in all countries find their just application in reference to every pupil of the Ursulines. The words were these : " I never knew a lady educated in an Ursuline Convent, who was not the instrument of diffusing piety and happiness around her."

CONCLUSION.

At the close of this third volume of the *Glimpses of the Monastery*, we owe our Readers an explanation, which, at the same time, must serve, in many ways, as an apology.

Undertaken at the voice of those who interpret for us the will of God; suspended or resumed at the same sacred signal ; accomplished during the intervals between the duties of the class-room, and the stated religious exercises of Convent-life ;—the humble *Gleaner* of the Cloistral Annals has not had, at her disposal, the leisure or repose that would have rendered her task at once easy and delightful.

We have written with a view to edify, rather than to please,—and for a class of readers on whose unlimited indulgence we could depend :—friends and relatives of the Ursulines of Quebec ; their pupils

of present or former times; friends of religion; or strangers to the Religious state,
whose curiosity we would gratify by
showing them something of that life so
unlike the world that it openly professes
to be " not of the world."

The dear and venerable name · of
MOTHER MARY OF THE INCARNATION
with which these pages commenced, has
been our talisman as we proceeded, and
in concluding we would seal with the
same our little offering —a labor of affection and gratitude as well as of duty.

Like that admirable servant of God,
may we and all who may peruse these
simple sketches, constantly aspire to the
only end of our existence, the attainment
of eternal happiness, through Him who is
" THE WAY, THE TRUTH, AND THE LIFE"—
through the ever ADORABLE HEART OF
JESUS!

TABLE

Of the Deceased Nuns of the Ursuline Convent, Quebec; from 1739 to 1875.

N. B.—The fifty-three Nuns who were living in 1739, are included in the list given in Vol. II of the Glimpses : the date of their decease being marked there, their names are not repeated here.

	Year of decease.	Age.
Rev. Mère Marie Françoise Cureux de St. Germain de St. Chrysostôme	1761	29
Marie Françoise Comparé de St. François Xavier......	1762	25
Marie Françoise Poulin dite Thérèse de St. Antoine....	1763	30
Geneviève Françoise de Lantaguac de St. Henri.......	1765	42
Angélique de Lantaguac de Ste. Marie...............	1769	39
Louise Françoise Soupirau de Ste. Ursule...............	1770	38
Angélique Charlotte Parisé de St. Jean-Baptiste........	1773	38
Charlotte Lefebvre de Ste. Geneviève...............	1778	55
Marie Joseph DesRoches dite des Anges..............	1781	58

Rév. Mère Marie Joseph Blais de St.
    Michel.................. 1782   38
Catherine Françoise Besan-
    çon de St. Joseph......... 1785   45
Marie Gilles de Landrière de
    St. Antoine.............. 1788   27
Marie Catherine Lagère de
    St. Gabriel.............. 1790   81
Marie Antoinette Poulin de
    St. François.............. 1790   67
Marie Charlotte de Varennes
    de Ste. Catherine 1792   31
Marie Apolline Marchand de
    St. Louis................ 1793   35
Marie Madeleine Massot de St.
    François de Paule 1794   61
Marie Geneviève Cureux de
    St. Germain de Ste. Pélagie 1796   51
Marie Jeanne Papin de St.
    Olivier.................. 1796   46
Marie Charlotte Brassard de
    Ste. Claire.............. 1797   67
Marie Elizabeth Richard de
    St. Augustin............. 1798   77
Madeleine Barthe de Ste Anne 1799   40
Marie Marguerite Davaune de
    St. Ls. de Gonzague...... 1802   83
Marie Josephte Méthot de l'In-
    carnation................ 1803   29
Marie Angélique Miller de St.
    Thomas 1804   36

. Mère Marie Elizabeth Blais de Ste.
Monique................ 1804 30
Marie Borne de St. Charles.. 1809 49
Marie Madeleine Cureux de.
St. Germain de Ste. Agathe 1811 75
Marie Louise Ignace DesRo-
ches de Ste. Angèle...... 1813 60
Marie Louise Gutké de St.
Stanislas.............. ..... 1814 26
Elizabeth Dougherty de St.
Augustin 1814 34
Marie Anne Brassard de Ste.
Madeleine............... 1815 79
Marie Marguerite Marchand
de Ste. Ursule........... 1815 61
Marie Elisabeth Delage de
St. Jean Baptiste......... 1819 69
Marie Josephte Lafontaine
dite Thérèse de Jésus.... 1821 65
Marie Ursule Blais de Ste.
Angèle 1822 26
Marie Anne Louise Tasche-
reau de St. François Xavier 1825 81
Louise Olivette Roy de St. Paul 1826 48
Marie Marguerite Coutant de
Ste. Anne............... 1826 48
Marie Angélique Vien de St.
Jean Chrysostôme....... 1826 1
Marie Thérèse Berthelot de
St. François d'Assise..... 1830 75

Mère Mary Ann Barber de St. Benoit	1848	38
Marie Anne Mathilde Painchaud de Ste. Antoinette..	1849	26
Françoise Elisabeth Giroux des Anges.............	1849	81
Marie Denise Talbot de Ste. Marguerite.............	1852	27
Marie Louise Oueille de Ste. Gertrude...............	1852	66
Marie Françoise Aubin de St. Antoine...............	1852	68
Marie Félicité Borne de St. Charles................	1853	69
Monique Plante de St. Stanislas	1860	28
Mary Henrietta McDonell de St. Aloyse..............	1860	30
Philomène Dion de Ste. Joséphine................	1861	25
Marie Elisabeth Sedilau dit Montreuil de St. Augustin	1861	74
Geneviève McKutcheon de Ste. Hélène.............	1861	72
Ellen Allan de Ste. Isabelle.	1862	26
Marie Marguerite Boissonnault de Ste. Monique....	1863	73
Henriette Cinnou de St. Alphonse	1864	42
Bridget McSweeney de St. Henri	1864	23

Rev. Mère Thersille Sénécal de Ste.
Clotilde................. 1873   29
Marie Félicité Boulé de Ste.
Elisabeth 1874   36
Isabella McDonnell de St.
Stanislas................ 1874   36
Marg. Cuddy de St. Athanase 1875   83
Clarence Legendre dite Marie
de la Nativité............ 1875   49

LAY-SISTERS.

Sœur Marie-Jeanne Bedard de St.
Hyacinthe.... 1760   47
Aug. Toupain de Ste. Marthe 1760   40
Marguerite Bédard de St.Denis 1767   40
Geneviève Ruëlle de St. Hy-
acinthe................. 1776   31
Gertrude Hamel de Ste. Anne 1778   45
Marie Clément de Ste. Véro-
nique................... 1780   23
M. Elizabeth Le Vasseur de
St. Ambroise............ 1784   68
Marg. Hamel de St. Alexis.. 1790   46
M. Angélique Déry de Ste.
Thècle.................. 1793   60
M. Rosalie Bédard de St. Fr.
Régis................... 1796   74
M. Marguerite Falardeau de
St. Laurent............. 1796   37

Sœur M. Anne Le Vasseur de St.
Ambroise 1800
M. Charlotte Chandonnet de
Ste. Claude 1804
M.-Madeleine Rousseau de St.
Clément 1801
Angélique Hamel de Ste. Mar-
guerite 1812
M.-Marguerite Hamel de Ste.
Croix 1817
M. Catherine Baudet de St.
André 1817
M.-Josephte Leclerc de Ste.
Thècle 1820
M.-Josephte Hamel de St. Hy-
acinthe 1823
Angélique Rousseau de Ste.
Marthe 1826
M.-Anne Ursule Nolette de
Ste. Croix 1834
Cécile Noël de Ste. Marguerite 1838
Geneviève Lacroix de St. Ni-
colas 1845
Judith Bilodeau de Ste. Rose. 1847
M. Françoise Berniche de St.
Hyacinthe 1857
Madeleine Boulet de St. Fr.
Régis 1857
M.-Françoise Leclerc de St.
Alexis 1859

Sœur M.-Françoise Fournier de St.
    Clément 1860   64
M.-Modeste Gagnon de Ste.
    Thècle 1863   61
Thérèse Couture de St. Denis 1864   73
M.-Anne Brière de St. Am-
    broise 1864   68
M.-Constance Lallier de St.
    Amable 1866   44
M.-Claire Lefèvre de St.Claude 1867   71
M.-Madeleine Bodin de Ste.
    Marthe 1868   63
Marguerite Sanfaçon de St.
    Antoine 1872   34
Luce Bouillé de St. Régis.. 1875   40

R. I. P.

PROFESSED CHOIR-NUNS ; 1875.

. Mère Adélaïde Plante de St. Gabriel,
    professed in 1815
Catherine Couture de Ste. Ursule.. 1818
Catherine Côté de Ste. Agnès.... 1818
Louise-Françoise Blais de Ste.
    Thérèse 1824
Anne Barber de St. François-Xa-
    vier 1828
Anne McDonnell de St.Jean l'Evan-
    géliste 1828
Christine Vermette de Ste. Angèle 1829

Rév. Mère Anne-Victoire White de Ste. J. de
Chantal 1830
M. J. de Chantal Letourneau de St.
Paul 1830
M. Thérèse Sherlock de Ste. Scho-
lastique 1831
Marie-Lse. Aylwiu de St. Philippe 1832
Marie Séraphine Truteau de Ste.
Anne. 1834
M. Joséphine Michaud de Ste. Cé-
cile.......................... 1835
Catherine Burke de St. Thomas... 1835
Catherine Murphy de Ste. Philo-
mène. 1838
Mary-Josephine Holmes de Ste.
Croix........................ 1840
Anne-Sophie Croteau de Ste. Ade-
laïde 1842
Marie-Caroline-Georgina VanFel-
son de St. Georges 1846
Marie-Christine Delorme de St.
Charles...................... 1846
Marie-Elizabeth Tims de St. Ca-
therine 1846
Catherine Gosselin de Ste. Claire.. 1848
Marie-Adèle Cimon de Ste. Marie 1850
M.-Lse. Stéphanie Proulx de Ste.
Julie........................ 1850
Marie-Henriette McDonell de St.
Aloyse....................... 1352

Rév. Mère Marie-Lse. Godbout de St. Pierre 1855
Olympe Gagnon dite Marie du Carmel 1856
Catherine Doherty de Ste. Christine 1857
Julie Thivièrge de Ste. Félicité.. 1858
Flavie Gagnon de Ste. Antoinette. 1860
Luce-Véronique Couture de la Vi-
    sitation....................... 1861
Johanna McDonald de St. Aloyse 1862
Léda Hardy de St. Augustin..... 1863
M.-L. O'Sullivan de Ste. Joséphine 1863
Marie-Malvina Gagné de St. Ra-
    phael......................... 1863
Hélène Joucas de St. Etienne.. 1864
Marie-Osité Faucher de Ste. Hé-
    lène.......................... 1866
Vitaline Dion de St. Henri....... 1867
Marie-Reine Girouard de Ste. Ger-
    trude......................... 1867
Emilie-Antoinette Routier de Ste.
    Cordule...... 1867
Odile-Luce Dion de Ste. Eulalie.. 1867
Emma Nault de St. Joseph....... 1868
Emma Cimon de St. Jean-Baptiste 1868
Célina Doré dite M. de la Présenta-
    tion.......................... 1868
Elmire Blanchet dite M. de l'In-
    carnation 1869
Adine Angers de Ste. Madeleine.. 1869
M.-Virginie-Clémentine de la Che-
    vrotière de St. Marc........... 1869

Rév. Mère Georgina Letourneau de l'Assomp-
tion 1869
Vitaline Gosselin de Ste. Pélagie.. 1870
Josephine Whaley. de St. Ignace.. 1871
Josephine Larose de Bon-Secours. 1871
Eveline Blanchet de St. Michel.... 1871
Marguerite McDonald dite M. du
Sacré-Cœur 1872
Marie-Stella Murray de St. Edouard 1872
Elise Gosselin de St. Frs. de Paule 1872
Emma Turcotte de St. Dominique. 1872
Malvina Pouliot de St. Alphonse.. 1873
Hélène Létourneau dite M. de la
Conception 1873
Henriette Audette dite M. de la Pro-
vidence 1874
Eléonore Lépine de St. Antoine... 1874
Mary-Ann McDonald de St. Benoît 1874
Paméla Roy de St. Louis........ 1874
Georgina Roy de Ste. Isabelle.... 1874
Alice Roy dite M. de l'Annonciation 1875

LAY-LISTERS.

Sœur Marie-Basile Ratté de Ste. Geneviève,
professed in 1822
Marie-Esther Turcot de Ste. Véronique 1843
Adélaïde Jacques de St. Laurent...... 1845
M. Hermine Biron de Ste. Candide 1847
Olive Fortin de Ste. Rose............ 1849

Sœur Marie Desharnais de Ste. Apolline..... 1849
Angèle Baillargeon de Ste. Luce...... 1851
Marie Bédard de St. François........ 1854
Caroline Blanchet de St. Alexis....... 1862
Philomène Sedileau Montreuil de St.
   Bernard......................... 1862
Aurélie Bouillé de St. Hyacinthe...... 1863
Marie Fournier de St. Clément........ 1864
M. Adéline Bertraud de St. Nicolas.... 1865
Mathilde Bergeron de Ste. Thècle..... 1866
M. Josephine Perron de St. Ambroise.. 1867
M. Elmire Naud de St. Denis......... 1867
Cézarine Bergeron de St. Amable..... 1869
Camille Tanguay de St. Claude....... 1870
Carôline Turgeon de St. Marthe 1871
Marie Gosselin de Ste. Germaine...... 1774
Marie Paradis de St. Roch............ 1874
Philomène Marcoux de St. Joachim.... 1875

APPENDIX.

A. *See page 36.—Version of the following :—*

1ère Bergère.

Changeons ici d'accords ;
Dieu ! quelle ardeur m'entraine
Qu'aperçois-je ?....Un Duquesne
Prend terre sur ces bords !
Autrefois, notre France
A ses nobles aïeux
Dut toute sa puissance :
Il vient par sa présence
L'affermir en ces lieux.

Chorus.

Que de son grand nom
Le beau vallon
Retentisse !
Joignons nos pipeaux
Aux chants nouveaux
Des oiseaux.
Que tous les coteaux
Tous les hameaux
Applaudissent !
Forçons les échos
A se mêler aux chants des chalumeaux !

2e.

Nos vœux ne sont pas vains ;
Bergers, sous un tel maître
Nous allous voir paraître
Les jours les plus sereius.
Nos campagnes fertiles
Dans le seiu de la paix,
Nos familles tranquilles,
Nos ennemis dociles :
Tels seront ses bienfaits.

3e.

Chers Bergers, fiuissons ;
Que le dieu de la lyre
A de plus forts, inspire
De plus nobles chansons.
Par ma bouche il s'exprime :
Dans cet auguste sang
Tout est trop magnanime,
Tout, trop grand, trop sublime,
Pour notre faible chant.

B. *Amicable relations between the Convent and the new government, page* 111.

It may not be uninteresting to iusort a little note written by Governor Murray to the Community, after his return to England.

It shows that if the English General kuew how to recoguize the services rendered to the sick and wounded of his army like a gentleman and a soldier; he could also acknewledge, as delicately as a lady, a slighter favor :

London, April 23rd 1767.

LADIES,

I have received the beautiful articles you had the kinduess to seud me : they are eertainly most acceptable in themselves, being the work of skilful and tasteful hands, but these gifts are especially precious to me ou accouut of the feeling that has dictated the offering. It is your esteem and attachment which I consider, and which I value as I ought. But this uew proof of your seutiments in my regard was not necessary to couviuce me that they were unalterable. During my sejouru in Canada, I had a thousand occasious of appreciating those kind feelings ; I am most sensible to the honor and it will ever be a pleasure to me to acknowledge the obligation.

I am persuaded you will continue to enjoy the tranquillity and happiness you merit : it is the recompense due to your virtues, and the fruit of your irreproachable life. It is these considerations that have won for you, Ladies, the esteem and confidence of all who kuow you. Coutinue to eujoy it. For my part, nothiug would give me greater pleasure than to have au opportunity to prove the high cousideratiou and attachment with which I have the honor to remaiu

Yours &c.,

Murray.

C. *Souvenirs of the different Sieges of Quebec.*
page 118.

It is not uncommon to meet with cannon-balls and bombs around the Convent-grounds. A few years ago, in repairing the roof of the *Sainte-Famille*, (the north part of the Monastery, occupied by the Community,) a cannon-ball was found still lodged between the roof and the wall. A bomb was lately found beneath the choir, buried in the earth : it had not exploded, and was still full of the materials with which it had been sent on its errand of destruction, whether by the English or by the Americans, cannot be said.

D. *Dark-days, page* 123.

From the letters of our nuns, as well as from history, we have gathered the following details of three *dark days*, not like those which were predicted but did *not* appear in 1873 ; for these did come, and terrified considerably.

On Sunday the 9th October 1785, after a night fearful as gusts of mind, claps of thunder and torrents of rain could make it, the morning was foggy. At about ten o'clock an easterly wind arose, when it suddenly became as dark as night for some minutes. This was followed by a thunder-storm and again by midnight darkness, thus alternating all the afternoon. People dined by candle-light. Our Nuns sang their Vespers with lights, as they are wont

to recite the evening Office. In the different churches
of the city, Divine Service had to be suspended till
lights were procured; and in private houses, the afternoon passed in lighting the candles and extinguish-
ing them. The recurring periods of total darkness,
or nearly total, lasted from seven to ten, or twelve
minutes. The two preceding days had presented
similar appearances, but of shorter duration.

No satisfactory solution has ever been given of
this extraordinary phenomenon. A similar *Dark-
Day* occurred, extending all over New England,
May 19th 1780.

E. *Three-Rivers, page* 193.

Three-Rivers is, at present, a thriving town,
having a population of 11,000 souls. It promises
to become a large city, by means of the country-
places around, and by the advantages of the North-
Shore Rail-Road.

It has a fine, spacious cathedral (1852) : and a college, with 218 students.

The Ursulines, from 1835 to 1873, have made the
important additions to their Monastery of two buildings,—80 and 90 ft. by 50.

F. *Visits, page* 208.

During several years [1814–1834], when first it
became customary for the citizens of the neighboring
Republic to visit Canada, Bishop Plessis and his

successors judged proper to permit the visit of the Monastery to such as came particularly recommended. The same privilege could not be refused to strangers from England in similar circumstances,—still less to the friends and relatives of the nuns on such occasions as Receptions, Professions, &c.

However agreeable or advantageous these visits may have been to the persons admitted, the nuns perceived plainly that these frequent interruptions of the Classes were detrimental to good order, as well as to the advancement of the pupils. It was, therefore, a measure which they heartily approved, when in 1834, the competent ecclesiastical authority decided that the rules of cloister should be observed.

We place here the correction of an error that occurs on *page* 210:—The portrait of Mother St. Henry which we possess is the *same* that was executed for Dr. McLoughlin of Paris. After the death of that friend and benefactor of the Ursulines of Quebec, the portrait was returned to us at the special request of his niece, Mother Josephine Michaud of St. Cecilia.

C. *page 233.*

The Ursulines of Charlestown, Mass.

In reserving a note here, it was our intention to give a succinct account of the foundation and the destruction of the Convent of Charlestown. But we

have found the subject treated in so satisfactory a
manner by the Editor of the *Charlestown Advertiser*
Boston, B.F. De Costa, Esq., that we would refer our
readers to his very interesting pamphlet, entitled
" Sister Sainte Claire." It is a sketch of the life of
this humble and pious Religious, a relative of the
able and impartial writer. We have also our thanks
to offer for his very amiable notice of the Glimpses,
of which he speaks as "thoroughly picturesque and
deserving to be read. "

The destination of the Ursulines left homeless on
the fatal 11th of August, we shall briefly state.

The youngest novice, Sr. St. Henry (Miss Cath.
Quirk) far gone in consumption, received a terrible
shock on the night the Convent was burned, and
died a few days later.

Three gave the remaining years of their lives to
the Ursulines of Quebec. The lay-sister, Grace
O'Doyle of St. Bernard died in 1838 ; Mother
Elizabeth Harrison of St. John, (who bore the name
of St. Joseph here) lived to serve her adopted Community thirty years ; Mother Mary Barber of St.
Benedict, but twelve. The memory of both is
cherished, not only by their sister-Religious, but
by all who ever had the advantage of being their
pupils.

Mothers St. Joseph (Miss O'Keefe) and St. Ursula
(Miss Chace) joined the Ursulines of Three Rivers ;
the former is living at this date ; the latter died a

few years ago, at the advanced age of 84. Mother Mary Augustine, (Miss Frances O'Keefe) and the two lay-sisters DeCosta of St. Clare, and Elizabeth Bennet of St. Ambrose, joined the Ursulines of New Orleans : the two latter, have since been called to their reward. Mother St. Augustine, has been appointed Superior of her Community several times, and occupies that office of trust and responsibility at the present date.

H. Page 240.

Mother Cecilia O'Conway, in religion Mother Mary of the Incarnation.

We subjoin, as a tribute of gratitude to a dearly beloved teacher, an extract from a letter, written the day after her death.—It was addressed to a member of another Community who had spent some days with us :—

..Our beloved Mother de l'Incarnation is counted with us no more ! To-morrow morning her dear remains will be laid in that lowly bed, where they will rest till the breath of the Angel's trumpet shall bid them rise to immortality. Dear blessed soul ! she had fulfilled a long career, and yet we hoped she would be spared a little longer. A few months ago she completed her seventy-sixth year. She had been visibly failing during the past twelve months, but we were so accustomed to see her pale emaciated

15

figure, that the change was not very striking. Her class-room was thronged as usual until the 16th December, when she was prostrated never to rise again. There has been, however, no particular malady, but rather a general decline, as of age and long infirmity, which at last ended in death. Wit the full use of her strong faculties, with that dept of piety for which she was so remarkable, she re ceived the last rites of our Holy Religion. She lin gered on till the 8th March, when at 11 o'clock i the evening, after a last Absolution from her Con fessor, and with a few watchers by her side, th feeble chord of life silently gave way—the gloriou day which knows no evening had dawned upon th trembling soul. "Blessed are the dead who die i the Lord : for they rest from their labours, and thei works do follow them.—"

Her works ! they were those of a life of sevent years. From her pious parents—of the old stock— she imbibed, even from the cradle, the swee milk of piety. At nineteen she had joined Mothei Seton in founding a Community which is now th glory of the Church in America. Disappointed, how- ever, in the Institution, which she had expected would have been a Monastery of Ursulines, she never ceased to sigh for the cloister. Bound by the strictest friendship to Mother Seton, she would not abandon the Institution during the life-time of the Foundress. From the time of that saintly woman's death, however, she renewed her entreaties to be alowed to follow the vocation which she felt was hers, nd at last obtained the coveted favor. In 1825, she vas admitted into the Novitiate of this house, and in 827, pronounced her vows with the satisfaction of me who at last has taken possession of an invaluable reasure.

During the forty-years it was given her to labor n the vineyard of the Lord as an Ursuline, she was n indefatigable teacher. It was truly the salvation f souls that was her point of view in everything. The lives of the Saints; pious and edifying exam- les, which she had witnessed; maxims of virtue he great truths of religion, of which she felt the brce in a most remarkable degree; these were with ler unfailing topics of conversation, which she knew low to vary, to adapt to the circumstances, and to ender effective. Her devotion to the Passion, to he Holy Infancy, and indeed to all the Mysteries of ur holy Religion, was unequalled. The Represen- ations of these holy scenes, in the Spanish taste, vere among the means she employed to impart a pirit of piety to the pupils. She was never too veary nor too occupied to undertake those pious de- orations, but she could not see them debased to a nere entertainment of curiosity. When she assem- oled the children around the crib and at the foot of he Cross, she wished them to meditate and pray. It was then her piety gave her eloquence and lent her strength. Few of the pupils who have spent a Christmas or a Holy Week here for the last forty years, will ever fail, as these Holy Anniversaries come round, to think of poor dear *Mère de l'Incarnation.*

Ursulines, Quebec.
March, 10th, 1865.

I. Page 248.

Visit of the Legislature, 1836.

The Ursulines, counting upon an indemnity fo; the loss of their property in France, had contracter debts in their late reparations for the Boarding School. At the same time the old building tha served for the Externs, was crumbling with decay and needed restoration.

In such circumstances, they made an application for pecuniary aid from the Legislature, and received the sum of $2000. It was an opportunity of whicl these Honorable Gentlemen took advantage to tes tify their esteem of the Institution, as follows :

"As a Boarding-School for young ladies, the Ur suline Convent is universally acknowledged to be one of the best in the country. These Religiou: ladies are entirely devoted to the education of young girls, and they have contributed greatly, from the earliest settlement of Canada, to form the manner and to engrave in the youthful mind the purest prin· ciples of morality, joined to habits of industry and order : nor have they ever demanded aid from the Legislature, &c.

Les Ursulines de Quebec, p. 676.

J. *Page 254.*

Examinations, at a recent date.

The *Morning Chronicle* has a detailed account of
recent "Prize Day", which we abridge, as fol-
)ws :—

This ancient, educational and religious establish-
ient has earned for itself during the course of many
ears—we were almost saying centuries—a world-
ride reputation, which is second to none for the ex-
ellent provisions there made for the highest ins-
ction and training of female children. Every
ar new laurels are obtained, and additional prestige
equired by the good ladies who superintend this
stimable work. In every quarter of the North
.merican continent there may be found ladies, lead-
rs of brilliant and intellectual social coteries, whose
quirements, accomplishments and refinement are
ue almost entirely to the devoted care paid to them
y the nuns of the Ursuline Convent of Quebec, in
eir maiden school-girl days..........,...

It-was exceedingly pleasant to find that the prizes
stributed by Madame Caron at the convent yesterday afternoon were as well merited as ever by the
fair contestants for knowledge, the same spacious
range of subjects, some of them abstruse and scien-
tific enough to frighten away male graduates In
spite of three powerful rival attractions, the halls of
the Ursuline Convent echoed to the tread of num-

berless feet a full hour and a half before the time
announced for the commencement of the programme.
Many who were not so desirous of choosing seats,
including a large contingent of parents, inspected the
lovely specimens of their daughters' skill which were
exhibited on tables arranged around one of the grat-
ed parlours of the convent.　Time would not permit
of a detailed inspection or any attempt at description
of this array of feminine handiwork.　There was a
veritable *embarras de richesses*, utterly confusing to
the male mind, entirely ignorant of that fine art which
from the earliest ages and pre-existent to painting,
sculpture or music, has given to woman a continuo
source of useful occupation for her working hou
as well as a pleasant amusement for her leisure
ones....Proceeding thence to the upper Hall, it now
being two o'clock, we found that Madame Caron,
accompanied by others of the Lieutenant-Governor's
family, escorted by Col. Amyot, A.D.C., had arrived.
She was introduced to the chair of honor by Mon-
signor Cazeau, Vicar General.　A lar uni of our
best known citizenesses, who ame in at the same
time, occupied places on the front seats.　Father
Lemoine, spiritual director of the Ursuline Convent,
Fathers Bonneau, Paquet, Vignon, Plamondon and
many others whose names we could not ascertain,
also took their places near the dais, which was
shortly afterwards taken up by the scholars who
filed in, as fair and fresh a bevy of young girls as
one would wish to see, all arrayed as they were in

their virginal robes of purest white, relieved only by
he color of the sash distinctive of the particular
order to which they belong.... Then came a distri-
ution of prizes by the Lady of the Lieutenant-
lovernor, she adding many encouraging words to
he gift when presenting it.... The Instrumental and
Tocal Music which composed the rest of the enter-
ainment was well selected and in every particular
admirably executed........ ::

The *Journal de Quebec* commences thus :—

DISTRIBUTION DES PRIX AU COUVENT DES URSU-
LINES DE QUEBEC.

Vendredi dernier a eu lieu, au couvent des Ursu-
ines, la distribution solennelle des prix aux élèves
ensionnaires de cette institution. Comme toujours
a grande salle avait peine à contenir les nombreux
parents et amis des élèves.

Tous les ans la même saison ramène la même
fête pourtant le public y revient toujours avec le
même emeut. Comment pourrait-il en être
autre songe à l'intérêt immense que
ous devons attacher l'éducation de la jeunesse,
t qu'on se rappelle la dette de reconnaissance que
otre bonne ville de Québec et le pays tout entier
ont contractée envers femmes dévouées qui con-
tinuent parmi nous ec tant d'éclat, l'œuvre com-
mencée, il y a plus de deux siècles, par la Mère M.
de l'Incarnation. Si les récompenses de la terre ont
peu de prix pour ces âmes d'élite, elles peuvent du

moins voir dans le respect dont on les entou
et dans la popularité de leur enseignement,
indice que leurs travaux n'ont pas manqué d'ê
appréciés. Eu nous invitant chaque année à vei
voir les triomphes de leurs élèves, elles nous foi
nissent l'occasion de constater qu'elles n'out pas fa
dans leur tâche. La séance de vendredi en est u
preuve éclatante............

Le programme était brillaut et comp
C'était uu vrai concert, dans lequel la c
tribution des prix aux diverses classes succéd
alternativemeut soit un chœur, soit un morce
d'orchestre dont l'exécution était parfaite. Tr
heures durant nous avons été sous le charme
cette musique, et des émotions qui accompagne
toujours ces fêtes, et chaque fois que les jeunes v
tuoses sout revenues sur la scène pour cherch
leurs récompenses, les applaudissements chaleurq
de l'auditoire leur out prouvé combien tous étaie
ravis de leur chaut, de leur bonne tenu

We take from the *Courrier du Ca*
date, the following :—

LES URSULINES DE QUEBEC.

Jeudi après-midi a eu lieu, dans la grande salle
du monastère des Ursulines la distribution solennelle des prix aux élèves pensionnaires et mi-peu-
siounaires de cette précieuse iution. Un public
d'élite s'était donné là rendez-vous.

Dans la salle, décorée avec une simplicité pleine

Milton Keynes UK
Ingram Content Group UK Ltd.
UKHW040926180224
437992UK00003B/75